Privacy and Data Protection Law in Mexico

Privacy and Data Protection Law in Mexico

Cristos Velasco
María Solange Maqueo

This book was originally published as a monograph in the International Encyclopaedia of Laws/Privacy and Technology Law.

Founding Editor: Roger Blanpain
General Editor: Frank Hendrickx
Volume Editor: Jos Dumortier, Pieter Gryffroy, Ruben Roex &
Yung Shin Van Der Sype

Wolters Kluwer

Published by:
Kluwer Law International B.V.
PO Box 316
2400 AH Alphen aan den Rijn
The Netherlands
E-mail: lrs-sales@wolterskluwer.com
Website: www.wolterskluwer.com/en/solutions/kluwerlawinternational

Sold and distributed by:
Wolters Kluwer Legal & Regulatory U.S.
7201 McKinney Circle
Frederick, MD 21704
United States of America
E-mail: customer.service@wolterskluwer.com

ISBN 978-94-035-0716-3

e-Book: ISBN 978-94-035-0856-6
web-PDF: ISBN 978-94-035-0866-5

The Authors

Dr Cristos Velasco is an attorney formed and trained in Mexico, United States, Spain and Germany with actual residence in Mannheim, Germany. His main areas of practice are global data privacy, cybercrime and cyber security law and policies. He is the manager of Evidencia Digital.LAT and Protección Datos México (ProtDataMx). He is currently External Law Lecturer at the Duale-Hochschule Baden-Württemberg (DHBW) Cooperative State University in Mannheim and Stuttgart, Germany and Senior Research Fellow and member of the Outreach Board Committee of the Center for AI and Digital Policy (CAIDP.Org).

Cristos currently teaches the courses: *'Information Technology Law'* and *'International Business Law & International Organizations'* at the International Business and Information Technology Division of the Duale Hochschule Baden-Württemberg Cooperative State University (DHBW) in Mannheim and Stuttgart, Germany. He has also lectured at the graduate level in many universities in Mexico, including CIDE, ITAM and UNAM. He is the author of the following books:

- *Aspectos Practicos de los Ciberdelitos y la Evidencia Digital (Practical Aspects of Cybercrime and Electronic Evidence in Co-authorship)*, Tirant lo blanch, February 2021.
- *Cyber Law in Mexico*, Wolters Kluwer Law & Business, Fourth Edition 2019.
- *Jurisdicción y Competencia Penal en relación al Acceso Transfronterizo en Materia de Ciberdelitos* (*Cybercrime Jurisdiction and Cross-Border Access)*, Tirant lo Blanch 2015.

Cristos holds a doctorate of laws *summa cum laude* from Universidad Carlos III of Madrid (UC3M) with specialization on cybercrime jurisdiction (2011); a Master's of Laws in International Trade Law (LLM) from the University of Arizona (2001), and a law degree from Universidad Del Valle de Mexico (1997). He holds five accredited international certifications in the fields of cybercrime, cybersecurity and data protection.

Cristos has served as an external consultant for international organizations, including the Inter-American Development Bank (IADB); the Organisation for Economic Cooperation and Development (OECD) (*Going Digital Project)*, INTERPOL (*ASEAN Cyber Capacity Development Project*); International Development Law Organization

(IDLO) and the Council of Europe (*GLACY+ Project),* the latter of which he has executed various capacity building activities on cybercrime and electronic evidence in countries of Latin America and the Caribbean (LAC) that are state parties to the Council of Europe's Budapest Convention on Cybercrime.

He has been an active member of the International Association of Privacy Professionals (IAPP) since 2014, where he has conducted training on the EU General Data Protection Regulation (GDPR) pursuant to IAPP's CIPP/E certification.

Dr Maria Solange Maqueo is currently director of the Legal Studies Division at Center for Teaching and Research in Economics (CIDE), member of the National System of Researchers with distinction by the National Council of Science and Technology (CONACYT), and member of the Advisory Council of the Mexican Bar Association Foundation, member of the Scientific Committee of the Tirant lo Blanch Publishing House, Editions of the University of Salamanca, the Editorial Board of the Academic Journal Studies in Information Law of the UNAM and the Advisory Board of the Network for Accountability. She was Former President of the Advisory Council of the National Institute for Transparency, Access to Public Information and Personal Data Protection (INAI).

María Solange has served as a member of the Judicial Processes Editorial Board of the newspaper *Reforma*, advisory board of Borde Político A.C. and the Internet.MX Association advisory board. She also has served as an external consultant for international organizations, including the Inter-American Development Bank (IADB), as well as the Council of Europe (*GLACY+ Project*) in order to promote and design legislation on personal data protection in Latin American countries.

She is the author of more than thirty national and international publications on the subject area. María Solange has also been a speaker at various forums throughout Mexico and in other countries, including Nicaragua, Colombia, Uruguay, USA, Canada, Spain, France, Tunisia and Sri Lanka. She has been a professor at several prestigious universities in Mexico and has more than fifteen years of teaching experience.

María Solange is a graduate of the Escuela Libre de Derecho and has a PhD in Law and Public Policies from the University of Salamanca, Spain and is a Jean Monnet scholarship recipient.

Table of Contents

Table of Contents

List of Abbreviations

ACHR	American Convention on Human Rights
AI	Artificial Intelligence
AI.MX	Asociación Mexicana de Internet (Mexican Internet Association)
AMLO	Andrés Manuel López Obrador
APEC	Asia-Pacific Economic Cooperation
Banxico	Banco de México (Mexico's Banking Central Authority)
CBPR	Cross Border Privacy Rules
CISEN	Center for Investigation and National Security
CNBV	Comisión Nacional Bancaria y de Valores (The Banking and Securities National Commission)
CoE	Council of Europe
CPTPP	Comprehensive and Progressive Agreement for Trans-Pacific Partnership
Condusef	Comisión Nacional para la Protección y Defensa de los Usuarios de Servicios Financieros (Commission for the Protection and Defence of Users of Financial Services)
Convention 108	Convention for the Protection of Individuals with regards to the Automatic Processing of Personal Data
CJEU	Court of Justice of the European Union
DOF	Diario Oficial de la Federación (Official Gazette of the Federation)
ECtHR	European Court of Human Rights
EU–Mexico Agreement	The Economic Partnership, Political Coordination and Cooperation Agreement between the European Community and Its Member States and the United Mexican States
FCC	Federal Criminal Code
FCCP	Federal Code of Civil Procedure
FCPL	Federal Consumer Protection Law

List of Abbreviations

Federal Constitution	Constitución Política de los Estados Unidos Mexicanos (Political Constitution of the United Mexican States)
FGR	Fiscalía General de la República
FLAP	Federal Law on Administrative Procedure
FLPPDPP	Federal Law on Protection of Personal Data for Private Parties
FLTAPI	Federal Law of Transparency and Access to Public Information
FLTB	Federal Law of Telecommunications and Broadcasting
FCAJ	Federal Court of Administrative Justice (Tribunal Federal de Justicia Administrativa)
FTL	Federal Telecommunications Law
GATS	General Agreement on Trade in Services
GLPPDPGPSI	General Law on Protection of Personal Data in Possession of Government and Public Sector Institutions
GLTAPI	General Law of Transparency and Access to Public Information
GPA	Global Privacy Assembly
G7	The Group of Seven
IACtHR	Inter-American Court of Human Rights
IFT	Instituto Federal de Telecomunicaciones (Federal Institute of Telecommunications)
INAI	Instituto Nacional de Transparencia, Acceso a la Información y Protección de Datos Personales (National Institute for Transparency, Access to Information and Personal Data Protection)
INE	Instituto Nacional Electoral (National Electoral Institute)
INEGI	Instituto Nacional de Estadística Geografía e Informática (National Institute for Statistics, Geography and Informatics)
INFOCDMX	Instituto de Transparencia, Acceso a la Información Pública, Protección de Datos Personales y Rendición de Cuentas de la Ciudad de México (Institute for Transparency, Access to Information, Personal Data Protection and Accountability)
INFOEM	Instituto de Transparencia, Acceso a la Información Pública y Protección de Datos Personales del Estado de México y Municipios
MXN	Mexican Pesos
NAFTA	North American Free Trade Agreement
NYCE	Normalización y Certificación Electrónica
OAS	Organization of the American States
OECD	Organisation for Economic Co-operation and Development

PGR	Former Office of the Attorney General
Profeco	Procuraduría Federal del Consumidor (Office of the Attorney General for Consumer Protection)
R3D	Red en Defensa de los Derechos Digitales
RFLPPDPP	Regulation of the Federal Law on Protection of Personal Data Held by Private Parties
RIPD	Ibero-American Data Protection Network
SAT	Servicio de Administración Tributaria (Tax Administration Service)
SCJN	Suprema Corte de Justicia de la Nación (Supreme Court of Justice of the Nation)
SCT	Secretaría de Comunicaciones y Transportes (Ministry of Communications and Transports)
SE	Secretaría de Economía (Ministry of Economy)
SFP	Secretaría de la Función Pública (Ministry of Public Administration)
SG	Secretaría de Gobernación (Ministry of State)
SHCP	Secretaría de Hacienda y Crédito Público (Ministry of Finances)
SIGER	Sistema Integral de Gestión Registral
TPP	Trans-Pacific Partnership
UMA	Unidad de Medida y Actualización (Measure and Actualization Unit)
UNESCO	United Nations Educational, Scientific and Cultural Organization
USA	United States of America
USMCA	United States-Mexico-Canada Agreement
WTO	World Trade Organization

List of Abbreviations

Foreword

In the development of modern law, the establishment of the right to privacy in Mexico is a relatively recent development. Nonetheless, the growing importance of privacy coupled with the development of new technologies and new business practices has placed privacy and data protection at the centre of the legal landscape in Mexico.

In this remarkably comprehensive overview, Velasco and Solange Maqueo have provided readers and law practitioners with the most updated information on legal and policy developments on privacy and data protection in Mexico. Their work provides the practical insight that is necessary to provide advice, to assess recent developments, and to identify new areas for legal developments.

Thanks to Velasco and Solange Maqueo, we can trace the development of the right to privacy in Mexico from the 2007 amendments to the Federal Constitution. As the authors explain, 'The Federal Constitution provides the legal foundation of private life and the right to data protection.' The authors also note that the right to privacy was established as the right to transparency was also strengthened, reflecting a paradox often found in democratic societies, and following the path of the United States which enacted a federal privacy law and strengthened the Freedom of Information in the same year. In the area of information policy, privacy of the individuals and the transparency of the government are the twin pillars of the modern democratic state.

Privacy law in Mexico has also pursued a path parallel to developments in the European legal system that established a right to informational self-determination in the famous German census case of 1983 carried forward to a fundamental principle in Article 8 of the European Charter of Fundamental Rights. In Mexico, the Federal Constitution in 2011 recognized the concept of 'habeas data', a similar effort to ground the right of individuals to control the use of their personal data in possession of others on a constitutional basis. As the authors note, Article 16 of the Federal Constitution also makes clear that privacy is an instrumental right that makes possible the enjoyment of other rights, including honour, self-reputation, and human dignity.

Mexico also exists within the legal obligations established by treaties and conventions, as well as the Inter-American Court of Human Rights. The authors note the global influences of these international legal frameworks and international institutions in the development of the right to privacy.

The text is well organized, and the summary of legal decisions provides citations for further reference. The text provides definitions for key terms in the data protection field, including lawful processing, data quality, purpose specification, proportionality, minimization, loyalty, accountability, and compensation when violations occur.

The authors also explore the emerging field of Artificial Intelligence (AI), noting that Mexico was one of the first countries to announce a national AI strategy, though progress on implementation has slowed. Mexico's data protection agency – the INAI – is a well-regarded organization that has contributed to global policy frameworks on AI and in 2021 hosted the annual meeting of the Global Privacy Assembly, the international network of Data Protection and Privacy officials. The INAI plays a critical role, upholding both rights of privacy and transparency across Mexico.

In their summary, Velasco and Solange Maqueo point to the opportunity to raise the standards for data protection in the digital environment and propose updates to regulate persistent identifiers, known as 'cookies', and for data protection for transborder data flows. They also call attention to the need for Mexico to align with the global frameworks for AI, such as the OECD AI Principles and the UNESCO Recommendation on AI.

Timely, comprehensive, authoritative, and thoughtful, Velasco and Solange Maqueo have provided a valuable overview of privacy and data protection law of Mexico.

Marc Rotenberg
Washington, DC
April 2022

Preface

This monograph on Privacy and Personal Data Protection in Mexico is one of the most complete and comprehensive legal studies in the field. On the one hand, it reflects the relationship of privacy as a fundamental human right with the current governing legal system in Mexico. On the other hand, it provides a comparative legislative tour and offers a broad jurisprudential and regulatory perspective which allows readers to understand how the interpretation and development of the right to informational self-determination and privacy have been achieved in Mexico.

Through this monograph, readers will learn the most recent legal developments in the field of privacy and personal data protection in Mexico, as well as relevant emblematic national cases brought to the national courts. This monograph covers a useful reference of more than forty federal laws that regulate different aspects concerning the processing of data, the right to privacy and confidentiality of information of individuals contained in files and public records. It also highlights outstanding conflicts and tensions with other fundamental rights, such as freedom of expression and access to public information.

This research developed by PhD. Maqueo and PhD. Velasco is an excellent contribution to the academic and research fields. The study compiles accurate and updated content for the specialized English-speaking community, while at the same time, it uses an easy and digestible approach for readers who wish to know more about the current legal situation, and the developments adopted regarding the protection of this fundamental right across Mexico. This monograph not only highlights progress in the exercise of these rights but also addresses the challenges and tasks that need to be forward within the legislative and jurisprudential field, namely having an independent data protection agency with sufficient autonomy and resources to enforce the law; the creation of a national privacy strategy sufficiently well coordinated with other data protection authorities around the world to facilitate and coordinate cross-border investigations while complying and navigating with the complexities of other data protection laws that need to be enforced in the private and government sectors.

The study here presented will undoubtedly be an international reference source for those who see privacy and the protection of personal data as a real possibility to demand respect for the dignity of the individual in the context of technological development.

Luis Gustavo Parra Noriega
Commissioner INFOEM
Metepec, Estado de Mexico
Mexico, April 2022.

General Introduction

1. The current monograph provides a general analysis of the current regulatory landscape in the area of privacy and data protection in Mexico. This monograph offers an overview and in-depth analysis of the regulatory framework on privacy and data protection, as well as recent updates on major policies, landmark cases and legal developments in this field in Mexico.

2. Two decades have passed since the receipt of the right to the protection of personal data in Mexico. Its evolution, initially applicable only to the public sector and in relation to the right of access to public information, has had a progressive direction. Currently, at a national level, México has a robust regulatory and institutional framework, with an independent data protection agency that has powers to prevent, investigate and sanction non-compliance with the principles and obligations of the right of personal data protection. In addition, the Mexican Constitution recognizes this right as an autonomous human right, although interrelated with the right to private life and privacy.

3. At the international level, there have also been significant advances. Mexico has signed several international human rights treaties and trade agreements related to privacy and personal data protection. In particular, Mexico's accession to the Convention 108 of the Council of Europe (CoE) in 2018 is a clear example of the relevance that the protection of personal data has gained in recent years for this country. Furthermore, at a regional level, updates have been made to the pioneering international instruments in this area, and others have been issued. This is the case of the *Standards for Personal Data Protection for Ibero-American States*, issued in 2017 by the Ibero-American Data Protection Network (RIPD), with the aim of establishing a uniform framework for the countries of the region, consistent with the European model that seeks to guarantee an adequate level of protection of personal data.

4. In addition, there is a growing body of jurisprudential precedents based on resolutions issued by the Supreme Court of Justice of the Nation (SCJN) and the Federal Courts, which provide greater interpretative criteria to delimit the scope of the rights to privacy and personal data protection, as well as its relationship with other human rights, such as freedom of expression and access to information. It is significant that the largest number of resolutions issued by Federal Courts in matter of personal data have been made in the course of the last three years.

5. The attention to the right of personal data protection in Mexico is consistent with the growing interest that the issue has aroused around the world since the enactment of the *General Data Protection Regulation (GDPR)* in the European Union. Due to the advance and changes in technology, like the deployment of services based on Artificial Intelligence (AI), the ongoing work of international organizations and the fact that a large part of the global population spends more time online as a result of the COVID-19 pandemic, either working from home, attending school or conducting businesses fully online, data protection has become more relevant than ever for the Mexican society.

6. Moreover, many challenges come within the protection of this fundamental right, in particular the enforcement of the law at the national level, having an independent data protection agency with sufficient autonomy and resources to enforce the law, a general national privacy strategy sufficiently well linked with other data protection agencies to facilitate and coordinate investigations at the global level in order to enforce data protection laws on a more coordinated basis against big companies, data brokers and other digital stakeholders with global presence.

7. The monograph here presented aims to provide readers and law practitioners with the most updated information on legal and policy developments on privacy and data protection in Mexico. The authors aim that the current monograph can be used as a useful and complementary source to provide and support legal services, fulfil regulatory compliance obligations, research and academic teaching, among other activities. This monograph does not cover theory, neither scientific proposals in the field. There are plenty of books and extensive literature not only in Mexico but also in countries of Latin America and Spain that fully address and cover said aspects. The approach of this monograph is more practical oriented as it seeks to fill an existing gap since there are no current specialized publications in English concerning the status quo of privacy and data protection regulation in Mexico.

General Background Information about the Country

§1. Historical and Societal Background

8. According to the etymology of the word, Mexico comes from the term 'metztli' (moon), 'xicitli' (centre) and the morpheme of place – 'co' (in, the place) which means: in the centre of the moon or in the centre of the lake of the moon.

9. The territory of Mexico was discovered more than thirty thousand years ago, and a large number of civilizations settled along the territory better known as the Valley of Mexico (Valle de Mexico). The Aztecs were among the most known of the civilizations of Mesoamerica that inhabited the said valley. In the year 1325, the Mexicans established the capital of the State known as Mexico-Tenochtitlan. In 1519, the Spanish conquerors arrived in Mexican territory. Following the conquest of Tenochtitlan, and settlement of the Spanish colony, the territory of Mexico was then known as New Spain. It was initially governed by Hernan Cortes, and subsequently ruled by the Spanish crown through a viceroyalty established in 1535.

10. After nearly three hundred years of Spanish domination, the independence movement commenced on 16 September 1810 under the leadership of Miguel Hidalgo y Costilla, a priest and José María Morelos y Pavón, a general. The act of independence was signed and acknowledged on 21 September 1821. The first constitution was enacted in 1824, and after several years of political struggles, invasion wars and territorial divisions, the constitution was modified to reflect the changes of a centralized republic into a federal republic in 1857.

11. Furthermore, after more than thirty-five years of dictatorship under the regime of former President Porfirio Diaz, and as a result of social and political inequalities among the population during the dictatorship period, the Mexican revolution movement began on 10 November 1910. After seven years of political conflict, wars, government reforms, former President Venustiano Carranza enacted the political constitution in the State of Queretaro on 5 February 1917, which is the current governing constitution of the Mexican Republic, which has been subject of more than 220 reforms and modifications till present.

12. Mexican culture is the result of a historic and sociologically complex process, which includes religious, economic and political issues, and assimilation of pre-Hispanic cultural elements, as well as the influence of external factors from other countries particularly from Europe and the United States. The cultural heritage, ethnic diversity and the traditions of the inhabitants, as well as its gastronomy, are some of the characteristics that Mexico proudly offers to the world. There are currently more than sixty-five ethnic groups, which represent more than 10% of the whole population. These ethnic groups still preserve their own language and traditions. Among the languages still preserved and spoken today are: Nahuatl, Maya, Zapoteco, Mixteco, Purepecha and Otomi. Mexico has more than forty thousand archaeological sites and historic monuments, many of which have been recognized as cultural patrimony of the nations by the United Nations Educational, Scientific and Cultural Organization (UNESCO).

13. The elected President for the period 2018–2024 is Andrés Manuel López Obrador (AMLO) from the left-wing political party Movimiento Regeneración Nacional. AMLO was a former Mayor of Mexico City between 2000 and 2005, and he was democratically elected as the President on 8 August 2018 after having participated three different times in the federal presidential elections from the year 2006. He took office on 1 December 2018 and will conclude his mandate on 30 November 2024.

14. Mexico is a free-market economy with one of the highest per capita incomes in nominal terms in Latin America, but one of the lowest per capita incomes across the Organisation for Economic Co-operation and Development (OECD) countries. Statistics from the National Institute for Statistics, Geography and Informatics (INEGI) estimates a total Nominal Gross Domestic Product of market prices equivalent to EUR 283,844 million for the third quarter of 2021. Annual inflation registered a record level of 7.68% in January 2022 due to the economic crisis caused by the COVID-19 pandemic; 3.54% in January 2021; and 3.24% in January 2020 according to statistics from INEGI.

15. Petroleum, manufacture and tourism are the main industries in order of importance. According to the World Tourism Organization, Mexico is the main travel destination in Latin America and the ninth most visited place in the world. According to statistics of the World Population Review, Mexico was ranked in the seventh place of the *Top 10 Countries Most Popular with Tourists* with around 45 million visitor arrivals in 2019.

16. The growth of migration in the last ten years has increased the remittances sent by migrants in the United States to their families and relatives in Mexico to the extent that such remittances are among Mexico's main sources of income, exceeded only by oil revenues. According to data of the World Bank, Mexico is the third-biggest remittance recipient in the world with around USD 43 billion in 2020 only preceded by China (USD 59.5 billion) and India (USD 83.1 billion). Family-related remittances are located among the five sources of national currency collection for the country, along with automotive exports, foreign direct investment, tourism and oil exports.

17. Mexico has been ranked in the thirty-fifth position of the World Happiness Report 2021, an index that measures the levels of happiness of 156 countries based on six key variables that support the well-being of individuals, namely: (i) income, (ii) healthy life, (iii) expectancy, (iv) social support, (v) freedom, (vi) trust and generosity.

18. Education and income inequalities continue to remain a problem, and it has worsened as a result of the economic turndown brought by the COVID-19 pandemic. Huge gaps exist not only between rich and poor but also between the north and the south, the urban and the rural areas. The informal economy of unregistered business and individuals is a very visible segment in the Mexican economy. According to the World Bank, the size of the informal sector accounts for slightly more than half of the total employment in the country.

19. Since the mid-1980s, Mexico has followed a neoliberal economic policy model with emphasis in the liberalization of trade with other countries. According to the Ministry of Economy (Secretaría de Economía (SE)), Mexico is one of the countries with the most commercial treaties in force, with a total of fourteen commercial treaties with fifty countries and thirty agreements for the reciprocal protection of investments with thirty-one countries and administrative regions and in addition to nine complementary trade agreements with countries of Latin America within the framework of the Latin American Integration Association (ALADI). Among the most notorious commercial treaties for the economy is the former North American Free Trade Agreement (NAFTA), which entered into force more than twenty years ago and that has recently been replaced by the United States-Mexico-Canada Agreement (USMCA). The USMCA is by and large the most important commercial partnership, nearly 90% of the exports go to the United States and Canada, and 55% of the total imports come from these two countries. Mexico signed the Trans-Pacific Partnership Agreement (TPP) on 8 March 2018. The TPP treaty aims to further liberalize trade and investment and consolidate the economic integration among twelve countries of the Asia-Pacific region without the support of the United States. The TPP, which was ratified by the Mexican Senate on 24 April 2018, covers a market of nearly 498 million people with a Gross Domestic Product per capita of more than USD 28,000, and it amounts to 13% of the global economy.

20. Likewise, Mexico is well positioned and is a member of a wide network of international and multilateral organizations. Mexico is a member of the United Nations since 7 November 1945; of the Organization of the American States (OAS) since its foundation on 5 May 1948; of the OECD since 18 May 1994; of the World Trade Organization (WTO) since 1 January 1995; of the Asia-Pacific Economic Cooperation (APEC) since 17 November 1993 and the ALADI since 12 August 1980.

§2. TELECOMMUNICATIONS INFRASTRUCTURE

21. The opening and liberalization of the telecommunications market in Mexico commenced in 1990 immediately after the privatization of Teléfonos de México (Telmex).[1]

The liberalization of telecommunications services and competition in different telecom sectors particularly among long-distance carriers commenced in 1995. Coincidentally, a year earlier in 1994, Mexico decided to reinsert itself into the global economy with the signature of the former NAFTA now the USMCA and the ratification of its membership to the WTO in 1995.

As part of Mexico's strategies to open the telecommunications market to competition, Mexico enacted in 1997 a federal telecommunications law – *Ley Federal de Telecomunicaciones* (FTL) – consistent with the compromises and commitments signed under the General Agreement on Trade in Services (GATS).

22. Since the privatization of Telmex in the early 1990s, that company has maintained a strategic de facto monopoly, particularly in local telephony and long-distance services. Telmex's monopoly on basic telephony officially ended in August 1996, when foreign licensed competitors were permitted by the Secretaría de Comunicaciones y Transportes – Ministry of Communications and Transports (SCT) – to begin operations across Mexico. Among the foreign competitors offering telephone services in the national territory are: Telefonica Movistar; Alestra, a subsidiary of AT&T; Axtel; Iusacell; Nextel; Maxcom; Unefon.

23. Simultaneously with the privatization of Telmex, the Mexican government issued concession titles to offer mobile telephony services and divided the country into nine different regions in order to spread such mobile telephony services, guaranteeing at least two operators in every region. However, as of today, there remain five mobile telephony providers that operate with their own network nationwide: (i) Telcel, controlled by the same corporate group as Telmex; (ii) Movistar, resulting from the takeover of the Mexican corporation Pegaso by the Spanish company Telefonica Movistar; (iii) AT&T Mexico; (iv) Iusacell, currently owned by Grupo Salinas; and (v) Unefon, controlled and owned by Iusacell and Grupo Salinas and operating under the network of AT&T.

24. Additionally, there are twelve virtual mobile operators that offer mobile telephony services: (i) Alo (operating under Telcel's network); (ii) Bueno Cell (operating under Telcel's network); (iii) Unefon (operating under AT&T's network); (iv) Weex (operating under Movistar's network); (v) QBOCEL (operating under Movistar's network); (vi) Maxcom (operating under Movistar's network); (vii) Megacable (operating under Movistar's network); (viii) Virgin Mobile (operating under

1. Telmex is the main national phone service provider. It was founded in 1947 and initiated as a private ownership company. The Mexican government acquired the company in 1972. Subsequently, the company was nationalized in 1976, and finally privatized in 1990. For more information about the history and development of Telmex, *see* Wikipedia available at: www.en.wikipedia.org/wiki/Telmex (last visited May 2022).

Movistar's network); (ix) Coppel (operating under Movistar's network); (x) Tuenti (operating under Movistar's network); (xi) Cierto (operating under Movistar's network); and (xii) Maztiempo (operating under Movistar's network).

25. From 1983 to 1995, satellite communications used to be a strategic activity reserved for the Mexican government for its exclusive development and control. Subsequently in 1989, the government incorporated TELECOMM, a national company formed exclusively for the operation of satellite and telegraph services across national territory.

26. The Political Constitution of the United Mexican States – *Constitución Política de los Estados Unidos Mexicanos* (Federal Constitution) was amended in 1995 in order to allow private sector participation in the offering and rendering of satellite communications services. The reform of 1995 responded not only to the demand of satellite capacity needed in Mexico but also due to the low and inefficient response from the government in providing and offering such satellite capacity.

27. The FTL of 1995 facilitated the granting of concession titles through a preliminary bidding process to private companies, in order to build and operate private satellites and to provide services in Mexico using foreign satellites with the express condition that its control and operations centre was located in Mexico and operated preferably by Mexicans. The FTL of 1995 also allowed SCT to grant concessions to issue and receive signals from foreign satellites that provide services in Mexico, so long as a bilateral agreement with the other nation allowed for reciprocity to Mexican satellites.

With the FTL of 1995, value-added services were also opened to competition, and in order to be offered as such, they were subject to registration before the now extinct Comisión Federal de Telecomunicaciones – Federal Telecommunications Commission (Cofetel). Currently, Telmex dominates the market of value-added services particularly Internet access through its service Infinitum, which currently holds more than 70% of subscribers accessing Internet through a telephone network and 40% of DSL users on the domestic market.

28. On 11 June 2013, former President Enrique Peña Nieto published a decree that amends eight articles of the Federal Constitution in matters of telecommunications – known as 'the constitutional reform on telecommunications' – which contains the most recent framework and obligations for telecommunications service providers operating in national territory and included the creation of a new telecom regulator known as 'Instituto Federal de Telecomunicaciones (IFT)' a regulatory agency currently in charge of supervising and enforcing the laws and regulations in the area of telecommunications, radio broadcasting and television services across national territory. The decree also establishes the creation of specialized tribunals in matters of economic competition, radio broadcasting and telecommunications by the Council of the Judicial Branch.[2]

§3. The Information and Communications Technology Market

29. The OECD reports that Mexico is among the largest producers and exporters of communications equipment in the OECD member countries, earning export revenues of USD 18,402 million during 2013 and USD 17,637 during 2012; and import revenues of USD 15,315 during 2013 and USD 13,641 during 2012, respectively.

30. The OECD Broadband Portal estimates that Mexico had a total of 23,113,472 fixed broadband subscriptions per 100 inhabitants by technology until June 2021. Mexico was ranked in thirty-seventh place of a total of thirty-eight countries members of the OECD.

In contrast, the OECD estimates that Mexico had a total of 107,934,820 mobile broadband subscriptions per 100 inhabitants by technology until June 2021. Mexico was ranked in thirty-third place of a total of thirty-eight countries members of the OECD.

§4. E-Government

31. The Coordinator of the National Digital Strategy of the Presidential Office[3] under the current administration of President AMLO published a decree in Official Gazette of the Federation (DOF) on 6 September 2021 that contains the *National Digital Strategy 2021-2024*.[4] The National Digital Strategy is a general roadmap for the entities and bodies of the Federal Public Administration, the main purpose of which is to guide and align technological and information security efforts and initiatives towards achieving a common goal and direction while attending internal needs and fulfil the demands and expectation of citizens. The objectives, lines of action and policies contained in the National Digital Strategy are aligned with the general policies established in the *National Development Plan 2019-2024*.

---

2. *See*: Decree amending and adding some provisions to Arts 6, 7, 27, 28, 73, 78, 94 and 105 of the Political Constitution of the Mexican United States in matters of telecommunications at: www.sct.gob.mx/fileadmin/GITS/Traducci%C3%B3n_Ingl%C3%A9s_Reforma_Const_Telecom.pdf (last visited May 2022).
3. The website of the Coordination of the National Digital Strategy of the Presidential Office is available at: https://www.gob.mx/cedn (last visited May 2022).
4. The *National Digital Strategy 2021-2024* is available at: https://dof.gob.mx/nota_detalle.php?codigo=5628886&fecha=06/09/2021#gsc.tab=0 (last visited May 2022).

as well as when it produces a criminal offense or disturbs the public order; the right to reply shall be enforced according to the law. The right to information shall be guaranteed by the State.

[Second Paragraph]

Everyone has the right to the free access to plural and timely information, as well as searching, receiving and disseminating information and ideas of any nature through any means of expression.

[Third Paragraph]

The State shall guarantee the right of access to information and communication technologies, as well as broadcast and telecommunication services, including bandwidth and Internet. For such purposes, the State will provide the effective competence conditions on the provision of said services.

For the purpose of this Article the following shall apply:

A. For the exercise of the right of access to information, the Federation and the States of the Federation, within the sphere of their respective jurisdictions, will be governed by the following principles and bases:

   I. All information held by any federal, state and municipality authority, entity, body, office and agency of the Executive, Legislative and Judicial Power, autonomous organizations, political parties, trusteeship, and public funds, as well as from any individual, company, labour union that receives and spends public sources or conducts authority activities in the federal, state or municipal sphere is public and shall only be reserved temporarily by public interest and national security reasons according to the terms prescribed by law. The principle of maximum publicity shall prevail in the interpretation of this right. Obliged entities shall document every act deriving from the exercise of their powers, jurisdiction or functions, the law shall determine the specific hypothesis under which the statement of inexistence of information may proceed.

   II. The information concerning private life and personal data will be protected under the terms and with the exceptions set by law.

   III. Everyone, without proving any interest or justifying its use, will have free access to public information, personal data or its rectification thereof.

   IV. Expeditious mechanisms for access to information and revision procedures shall be established. These procedures will be brought before specialized autonomous organizations and impartial agencies established under this constitution.

   V. The obliged entities shall keep their documents on administrative updated files. They shall publish through available electronic means the complete and updated information about their management indicators and exercise of public resources that allow for the accountability and the compliance of their objectives and the obtained results.

   VI. The laws will define the way in which obliged entities shall make public the information related to public resources delivered to companies or individuals.

VII. Failure to comply with the provisions on public information access will be punished under the terms set by the laws.
VIII. […]

Article 16

[First Paragraph]
No person shall be in his private affairs, family, home address, paperwork or possession invaded, without a written order from a competent authority, duly explaining the legal cause of the proceeding. In the trials and procedures followed in the form of a trial in which orality is established as a rule, it will be sufficient to acknowledge them through any medium that offers certainty of its content and compliance with the provisions of this paragraph.
[Second Paragraph]
Every individual has the right to the protection of his personal data, and to access, correct and cancel such data. Every individual has the right to oppose disclosure of his data, according to the law. The law shall establish exceptions to the criteria that rule the principles governing data processing, due to national security reasons, law and order, public security, public health, or for the protection of third party's rights.
[Twelfth Paragraph]
Private communications shall not be breached. The law shall punish any action against the liberty and privacy of such communications, except when they are voluntarily given by one of the individuals involved in them. The judge shall assess the implications of such communications, provided they contain information related to the perpetration of a crime. Communications that violate the duty of confidentiality established by law shall not be admitted in any case.
[Thirteenth Paragraph]
Only the federal judicial authority can authorize the interception of private communications, at the request of the respective federal authority or the Head of the Public Prosecutor Office of the respective State. The authority that makes request shall present in writing the legal causes for the request, describing therein the kind of interception required, the individuals subjected to interception and the term thereof. The federal judicial authority cannot authorize the interception of private communications when the matters involved deal with electoral, fiscal, commercial, civil, labor or administrative subjects, and for communications between the defendant with his defence attorney.
[Fifteenth Paragraph]
The authorized interventions shall be subjected to the requirements and limitations set forth in the laws. The results of interception of communications that do not comply with the aforesaid requirements will not be admitted as evidence.
[Seventeenth Paragraph]
The sealed correspondence circulating through couriers shall be exempt from any search and the violation thereof shall be punishable by the law.

Likewise, it is worth noting that each of the thirty-two States of the Mexican Republic has its own constitution, which mirrors to a certain extent the provisions on civil liberties of the Federal Constitution with some minor differences.[8]

§1. National Case Law on Privacy and Data Protection

38. The first jurisprudential theses on the protection of personal data ruled by Federal Courts refer to the provisions contained in the Federal Law of Transparency and Access to Governmental Public Information (FLTAGPI), currently abrogated, on the confidentiality and security of personal data. In particular, the first criterion, issued in August 2004, refers to the obligation to adopt security measures by the economic competition authority, in order to guarantee the security of data and avoid the alteration, loss, transmission and unauthorized access to confidential information of economic agents, during investigation procedures for absolute monopolistic practices.[9] Currently, there are more than 150 criteria on the right to personal data protection.

39. It was not until 2011 that the first jurisprudential thesis was issued regarding the right to the protection of personal data as a human right recognized by the Mexican Constitution. This criterion refers to the habeas data action to exercise the rights of access, rectification, opposition and cancellation of personal data, provided for in Article 16 of the Federal Constitution.[10] From that year onwards, Federal Courts significantly increased the number of decisions concerning personal data protection. In this regard, Federal Courts issued a ruling in which it held the criterion that personal data subjects not only have the right to oppose the disclosure of their personal data in the public versions prepared by governmental authorities, but also with respect to the information that concerns individuals. In this case, Federal Courts held that data subjects have the right to intervene in the delimitation or determination of the information that is intended to be disclosed. Thus, courts (at a federal level) recognize de facto a legal interest to challenge such kind of decisions.[11]

40. In their most recent resolutions, Federal Courts have defined the right to the protection of personal data, provided for in Articles 6 and 16 of the Federal Constitution, as the right of each individual to control the access and use of their own

8. The full text of the States Constitutions is available in Spanish in the website of the Supreme Court of Justice at: https://www.sitios.scjn.gob.mx/centrodedocumentacion/node/91.
9. Seventh Collegiate Court on Administrative Matters of the First Circuit, Ninth Epoch, Register 180940, Thesis I.7o.A.312 A, Federal Weekly Judiciary Gazette, Volume XX, August 2004, p. 1565. Available at: https://sjf2.scjn.gob.mx/detalle/tesis/180940.
10. Fourth Collegiate Court on Administrative Matters of the First Circuit, Ninth Epoch, Register 160980, Thesis I.4o.A.790 A, Federal Weekly Judiciary Gazette, Volume XXXIV, September 2011, p. 2244. Available at: https://sjf2.scjn.gob.mx/detalle/tesis/160980.
11. Plenary of Circuits on Administrative Matters of the First Circuit, Tenth Epoch, Register 2006753, Jurisprudence PC.I.A. J/12 K (10a.), Federal Weekly Judiciary Gazette, Book 7, Volume II, June 2014, p. 1127. Available at: https://sjf2.scjn.gob.mx/detalle/tesis/2006753.

information, in order to protect the right to private life.[12] In this regard, the SCJN has resolved that the main purpose of the legislation on personal data protection is to guarantee privacy and the right to informational self-determination.[13]

41. In accordance with Article 16 of the Federal Constitution, Federal Courts have resolved and linked the personal data protection to the enjoyment of other fundamental rights, such as the right to honour, self-reputation and human dignity.[14]

42. Despite the right to personal data protection was initially oriented to safeguard privacy and informational self-determination of natural persons, in early times, the SCJN has ruled that this right provided for in Articles 6 and 16 of the Federal Constitution can be recognized as corporate entities with respect to the confidentiality of their address and communications, economic, commercial or identity reports.[15] This criterion is based, among other things, on a pro person interpretation of human rights provided for in Article 1 of the Federal Constitution.

Additionally, the SCJN has said that 'the assets protected by the right to privacy and personal data protection of legal entities, comprise those documents and information that are inherent to them, which must remain outside the knowledge of third parties', regardless of the principle of maximum publicity provided for in Article 6 of the Mexican Constitution. In that sense, the information delivered to authorities by corporate entities is confidential when it is private because it contains data that could be equated to personal data.[16] By and large, the right of corporate entities to the confidentiality of their information is not absolute; it is subject to the limits and restrictions provided for by law. An example of their limits can be found in corporations that have been sanctioned by economic competition authorities for absolute

12. Third Collegiate Court on Civil and Work Matters of the Fifth Circuit, Tenth Epoch, Register 2021523, Thesis V.3o.C.T.10 K (10a.), Federal Weekly Judiciary Gazette, Book 74, Volume III, January 2020, p. 2445. Available at: https://sjf2.scjn.gob.mx/detalle/tesis/2021523.
13. National Supreme Court of Justice, Tenth Epoch, Register 2022917, Jurisprudence 2a./J. 10/2021 (10a.), Federal Weekly Judiciary Gazette, Book 84, Volume II, March 2021, p. 1651. Available at: https://sjf2.scjn.gob.mx/detalle/tesis/2022917.
14. Tenth Collegiate Court on Administrative Matters of the First Circuit, Tenth Epoch, Register 2020563, Thesis I.10o.A.5.CS (10a.), Federal Weekly Judiciary Gazette, Book 70, Volume III, September 2019, p. 2199. Available at: https://sjf2.scjn.gob.mx/detalle/tesis/2020563.
15. This criterion has been gradually modified, since initially the right to the protection of personal data was only recognized for natural persons. In this regard *see:* Third Collegiate Court of the Thirteenth Circuit, Ninth Epoch, Register 176077, Thesis XIII.3o.12 A, Federal Weekly Judiciary Gazette, Volume XXIII, January 2006, p. 2518. Available at: https://sjf2.scjn.gob.mx/detalle/tesis/176077; National Supreme Court of Justice, Ninth Epoch, Register 169167, Thesis 2a. XCIX/2008, Federal Weekly Judiciary Gazette, Volume XXVIII, July 2008, p. 549. Available at: https://sjf2.scjn.gob.mx/detalle/tesis/169167; and National Supreme Court of Justice, Tenth Epoch, Register 2005521, Thesis P. I/2014, Federal Weekly Judiciary Gazette, Book 3, Volume I, February 2014, p. 273. Available at: https://sjf2.scjn.gob.mx/detalle/tesis/2005521.
16. National Supreme Court of Justice, Tenth Epoch, Register 2005522, Thesis P. II/2014 (10a.), Federal Weekly Judiciary Gazette, Book 3, Volume I, February 2014, p. 274. Available at: https://sjf2.scjn.gob.mx/detalle/tesis/2005522.

monopolistic practices, where in many cases, their identity and liability are not protected, considering that this information is necessary to protect the rights of third parties, such as the right to obtain a compensation of the damages caused.[17]

43. The SCJN as well as Federal Courts have had the opportunity to analyse the relationship and conflict between the right to personal data protection and the right of access to public information, in ponderative terms. In this regard, the SCJN recognizes that 'the right to access to public information governs as general rule, although limited, also in a generic way, by the right to the protection of personal data'. Consequently, 'public access –for all people regardless of the interest they may have – to personal data other than those of the information petitioner himself only comes in certain cases, expressly recognized by the respective laws'.[18]

As an example of the latter, Federal Courts have ruled that the information of taxpayers, whose tax credits have been condoned, is public. Thus, the authorities that must provide this information are not obliged to obtain the consent of the taxpayers who have received this tax benefit since they do not have an enforceable right, given the public nature of that information.[19]

44. In order to determine in which cases Mexican legislation on personal data protection is applicable to Internet search engines on the Internet, Federal Courts have ruled that the licence to use a trademark sign, granted by a foreign company in favour of a Mexican company, is a sufficient reason to consider its application to the licensed company.[20]

---

17. First Collegiate Court on Administrative Matters of the First Circuit, Specialized in Economic Competition, Broadcasting and Telecommunications, Tenth Epoch, Register 2011916, Thesis I.1o.A.E.159 A, Federal Weekly Judiciary Gazette, Book 31, Volume IV, June 2016, p. 2872. Available at: https://sjf2.scjn.gob.mx/detalle/tesis/2011916.
18. National Supreme Court of Justice, Tenth Epoch, Register 2000233 Thesis 1a. VII/2012 (10a.), Federal Weekly Judiciary Gazette, Book V, Volume I, February 2012, p. 655. Available at: https://sjf2.scjn.gob.mx/detalle/tesis/2000233.
19. Plenary of Circuits on Administrative Matters of the First Circuit, Tenth Epoch, Register 2020687, Jurisprudence PC.I.A. J/153 A (10a.), Federal Weekly Judiciary Gazette, Book 70, Volume II, September 2019, p. 1340. Available at: https://sjf2.scjn.gob.mx/detalle/tesis/2020687.
20. Tenth Collegiate Court on Administrative Matters of the First Circuit, Tenth Epoch, Register 2020549, Thesis I.10o.A.120. A (10a.), Federal Weekly Judiciary Gazette, Book 70, Volume III, September 2019, p. 1853. Available at: https://sjf2.scjn.gob.mx/detalle/tesis/2020549.

Chapter 2. National Application of Regional and International Conventions (Including, E.g., National Jurisprudence Regarding ECHR Article 8 and Judgments of the ECtHR Regarding Violations of Article 8 by the Country)

§1. International Treaties and Conventions

45. Under Mexican law, international treaties and conventions are hierarchically superior to federal and state laws, but they have an inferior hierarchy with respect to the Federal Constitution.[21]

In accordance with Article 1 of the Federal Constitution, in relation to Article 133 of said Fundamental Norm, the SCJN has adopted the criterion that 'there is a joint recognition of human rights whose sources are the Constitution and the international treaties to which the Mexican State is a party'. In this regard, the SCJN has stated that 'human rights, regardless of their source, constitute the control parameter of constitutional regularity, according to which the validity of all the norms and acts of authority that form part of the legal system shall be analyzed'. Consequently, in the Mexican legal system, pursuant to the criterion of the SCJN, 'human rights standards, regardless of their source, are not related in hierarchical terms, however, when the Constitution establishes an express restriction on the exercise of the human rights it will have to be pursuant to what the constitutional norm indicates'.[22]

In this context, the determination of the content and scope of human rights must be carried out in accordance with both the Federal Constitution and international treaties ratified by Mexican Congress, privileging at all times the interpretation that provides individuals with the broadest protection in application of the *pro personae* principle recognized by Article 1 of the Federal Constitution. However, 'when there is an express restriction on the exercise of a human right in the Constitution, it must comply with what the constitutional norm indicates'.[23]

46. Mexico has signed and ratified the following international conventions that contain provisions on the right to private life and protection privacy rights, although they do not specifically apply to the digital context:

---

21. Mexico's Supreme Court of Justice issued a landmark jurisprudence in November 1999 resolving the current hierarchy of international treaties and conventions within the legal system as part of the interpretation of Art. 133 of the Federal Constitution. *See* National Supreme Court of Justice, Ninth Epoch, Register 192867, Thesis P. LXXXVII/99, Federal Weekly Judiciary Gazette Volume X, November 1999. Available at: https://sjf2.scjn.gob.mx/detalle/tesis/192867.
22. SCJN, Contradicción de Tesis 293/2011, Pleno, Min. Arturo Zaldívar, resolución del 3 de septiembre de 2013. The text of the resolution is available in Spanish in the website of the Supreme Court of Justice at: https://www2.scjn.gob.mx/asuntosrelevantes/pagina/seguimientoasuntosrelevantespub.aspx?id=129659&seguimientoid=556#:~:text=SE%20UBICAN%20JER%C3%81RQUICAMENTE%20POR%20ENCIMA,por%20debajo%20de%20la%20Constituci%C3%B3n.
23. SCJN, Tesis 1ª./J. 29/2015 (10ª.), *Gaceta del Semanario Judicial de la Federación*, Libro 17, Abril de 2015, Tomo I, p. 240. Available in Spanish at: https://sjf2.scjn.gob.mx/detalle/tesis/2008935.

(i) Universal Declaration of Human Rights (1948) [Article 12].
(ii) American Declaration of Rights and Duties of Mankind (1948) [Articles 5, 9 and 18].
(iii) The International Pact of Civil and Political Rights (1966) [Article 17].
(iv) The American Convention of Human Rights (1969), better known as the Pact of San José, Costa Rica [Article 11].
(v) The Convention on the Rights of the Children (1989) [Article 16].
(vi) The International Convention on the Protection of the Rights of All Migrant Workers and Members of Their Families (1990) [Article 14].

47. The right to respect for private life is regulated under Article 11 of the *American Convention on Human Rights* better known as the '*Pact of San Jose*'.[24] Article 11 regulates the protection of honour and dignity of individuals in general. Section 2 of Article 11 specifically establishes that '*No one may be the object of arbitrary or abusive interference in his private and family life, in his home or in his correspondence, nor of illegal attacks against his honor or reputation.*' Section 3 of Article 11 stipulates that '*everyone has the right to the protection of the law against such interference or attacks*'. Unlike the Charter of Fundamental Rights of the EU (Article 8), the *American Convention on Human Rights* does not regulate the right to the protection of personal data.

The Convention establishes two main institutions, the *Inter-American Commission of Human Rights* and the Inter-American Court of Human Rights (IACtHR), which are the competent entities of the Inter-American System on Human Rights responsible for receiving and hearing complaints and resolving disputes concerning the fulfilment of the commitments made by State parties under the *American Convention on Human Rights*.

48. Mexico ratified the *American Convention on Human Rights* on 2 March 1981, and recognized the jurisdiction of the IACtHR on 16 December 1998.[25]

49. In accordance with the Mexican Supreme Court of Justice resolving the contradiction of rulings 293/2011, the interpretative criteria included in the resolutions

24. The *American Convention on Human Rights* was adopted on 22 Nov. 1969 in the city of San Jose, Costa Rica, and it has been in force since 18 Jul. 1978. Only twenty-four states have ratified this convention and is available at: https://www.corteidh.or.cr/tablas/17229a.pdf.

This convention is the equivalent of the European Convention on Human Rights for the Americas. However, the scope of the jurisprudence from the Inter-American Court on Human Rights concerning the interpretation of Art. 11 on the right to private and family life has been somehow limited compared to the cases and jurisprudence of the European Court of Human Rights concerning the application of Art. 8 of the European Convention on Human Rights. These asymmetries are especially evident in the relation between the right to private life and personal data protection. At the time of the publication of this monograph, the Inter-American Court on Human Rights has not yet issued cases or jurisprudence concerning specifically to the right to personal data protection right.

25. See the chart of signatures and ratifications.

of the IACtHR are binding for the judicial system in Mexico, even in those cases in which this country has not been a party.[26]

50. Further, Mexico signed and ratified the following conventions and implemented relevant guidelines that deal more specifically with the processing of personal information, data and files contained in electronic form and the regulation of transborder flows of personal data:

(i) United Nations Guidelines for the Regulation of Computerized Personal Data Files of 21 July 1988.[27]
(ii) International Standards on the Protection of Personal Data and Privacy (The Madrid Resolution of November 2009).[28]
(iii) The OECD Revised Guidelines on the Protection of Privacy and Transborder Flows of Personal Data (2013).[29]
(iv) APEC Privacy Framework (2015).[30]
(v) The CoE Convention for the Protection of Individuals with regards to the Automatic Processing of Personal Data (Convention 108).[31]

51. Mexico ratified Convention 108 on 28 September 2018.[32] As of the date of this monograph, Mexico has not yet signed Convention 108+. It is worth mentioning that during data protection day 2021 that marked the fortieth anniversary of Convention 108, the CoE organized a conference on data protection day in Latin America with the participation of national data protection authorities of Argentina, Costa Rica, Colombia, Mexico and Uruguay. The representatives of INAI announced that Mexico will shortly be requesting accession to Convention 108+, as well as adequacy status from the European Commission under the GDPR.[33]

§2. Cases and Jurisprudence of the IACtHR

52. Until June 2021, the IACtHR has issued forty-four judgments regarding the scope of interpretation of Article 11 of the American Convention on Human Rights

26. Mexican Supreme Court of Justice, Contradicción de Tesis 293/2011, pp. 54-66, available at: https://www.scjn.gob.mx/derechos-humanos/sites/default/files/sentencias-emblematicas/sentencia/2020-12/CT%20293-2011.pdf.
27. Available at https://digitallibrary.un.org/record/43365?ln=en.
28. Available at: https://bit.ly/3lvo5yD.
29. Available at https://www.oecd.org/digital/ieconomy/privacy-guidelines.htm.
30. Available at: https://www.apec.org/Publications/2017/08/APEC-Privacy-Framework-(2015).
31. Convention 108 is available at: https://www.coe.int/en/web/conventions/full-list/-/conventions/treaty/108.
32. *See 'Decreto Promulgatorio de la Presidencia de la Republica'* published in DOF on 28 Sep. 2018, available at: https://dof.gob.mx/nota_detalle.php?codigo=5539474&fecha=28/09/2018.
33. Council of Europe, '*Data Protection Day 2021 in Latin America. 40th Anniversary of data protection Convention 108*', available at: https://www.coe.int/en/web/data-protection/dpd2021-in-latin-america.

(ACHR) out of a total of 424 judgments.[34] It has also issued an Advisory Opinion with respect to this article, referred to 'Gender, Identity, and Equality and Non-Discrimination of Same-Sex Couples'.[35]

53. In its Spanish version, Article 11 of the ACHR is entitled 'Protección de la Honra y la Dignidad' (protection of honour and dignity).[36] It explains why in its first judgments related to Article 11, the Court dealt with the right of honour and reputation of people unjustly accused in public of different types of crimes.[37] In this regard, the Court has reiterated in its jurisprudence that 'a judicial proceeding does not constitute, in itself, an unlawful attack on the honor or dignity of a person. The proceeding serves to resolve a dispute, even though it may indirectly cause annoyance to those who are subject to the prosecution. Moreover, it is almost inevitable that this should be so; to the contrary, the practice of contested lawsuits would be totally excluded'.[38] However, despite the heading of Article 11 of the ACHR, the IACtHRs has observed that this provision 'has a widen content that include the protection of the home, the private life, the family and the correspondence'.[39]

54. The first judgment in which the IACtHR addresses 'the right to private life', beyond the right to honour and dignity, is the case of the *Ituango Massacres v. Colombia* in 2006. From this paradigmatic case, the IACtHR has held that 'Article 11(2) of the ACHR protects an individual´s private life and home from arbitrary or abusive interference. It recognizes that there is a personal sphere that must be protected from interference by outsiders and that personal and family honor and the home must be protected against such interference.'[40] Moreover, the IACtHR has observed that 'the sphere of privacy is characterized by being exempt from and immune to abusive and arbitrary invasion or attack by third parties or the public

---

34. Cfr. Judgments of the Inter-American Court of Human Rights. Available at: https://www.corteidh.or.cr/casos_sentencias.cfm?lang=en.
35. Inter-American Court of Human Rights, Advisory Opinion OC-24/17 of 24 Nov. 2017, Series A No. 24. Available at: https://www.corteidh.or.cr/docs/opiniones/seriea_24_eng.pdf.
36. Paradoxically, in its English version the translation of Art. 11 of the ACHR is not literal. In this version, it is entitled 'Right to privacy'. Cfr. https://www.cidh.oas.org/basicos/english/basic3.american%20convention.htm.
37. Cfr. Inter-American Court of Human Rights. Case of *Cesti-Hurtado v. Peru*, Judgment of 29 Sep. 1999, para. 177; Case of the *Gómez Paquiyauri Brothers v. Peru*, Judgment of 8 Jul. 2004, p. 182; among others.
38. Inter-American Court of Human Rights. Case of *Cesti-Hurtado v. Peru*, Judgment of 29 Sep. 1999 (Merits), para. 177. Available at: https://www.corteidh.or.cr/docs/casos/articulos/seriec_56_ing.pdf. This jurisprudence has been restated by the Court in other cases: Case *Bueno Alves v. Argentina*, Judgment of 11 May 2007, para. 122; and Case *Valle Jaramillo et al. v. Colombia*, Judgment of 27 Nov. 2008, para. 176.
39. Inter-American Court of Human Rights. Case of *Escué-Zapata v. Colombia*, Judgment of 4 Jul. 2007 (Merits, Reparations and Costs), para. 91. Available at: https://www.corteidh.or.cr/docs/casos/articulos/seriec_165_ing.pdf. This jurisprudence has been restated by the Court in other cases, such as: *Fernández Ortega et al. v. Mexico*, Judgment of 30 Aug. 2010, para. 129; and Case *Fernández Prieto and Tumbeiro v. Argentina*, Judgment of 1 Sep. 2020, para. 102.
40. Inter-American Court of Human Rights. Case of the *Ituango Massacres v. Colombia*, Judgment of 1 Jul. 2006 (Preliminary Objections, Merits, Reparations and Costs), para. 193. Available at: https://www.corteidh.or.cr/docs/casos/articulos/seriec_148_ing.pdf.

authorities. In this regard, an individual's home and private life are intrinsically connected, because the home is the space in which private life can evolve freely'.[41]

55. The IACtHR has extended the scope of the right to privacy to areas other than those explicitly provided under Article 11 of the ACHR such as family home and correspondence. This is the case of other forms of private communications, like telephone conversations.[42] Moreover, the IACtHR has held that 'Article 11 applies to telephone conversations irrespective of their content and can even include both, the technical operations designed to record this content by taping it and listening to it, or any other element of the communication process. For example, the time and duration of the calls that are made, the identity of the speakers, the frequency, time and duration of the calls, aspects that can be verified without the need to record the content of the call by tapping the conversation.'[43] The extension of the scope of Article 11 is consistent with the idea of applying this provision to technological advancements, their increased use and the State obligation 'to adapt the traditional forms of protecting the right to privacy to current times'.[44]

56. The IACtHR has resolved that 'the right to privacy is not an absolute one, and, so, it may be restricted by the States provided that their interference is not abusive or arbitrary; accordingly, such restriction must be statutorily enacted, serve a legitimate purpose, and meet the requirements of suitability, necessity, and proportionality which render it necessary in a democratic society'.[45]

57. According to settled case law of the IACtHR, 'the concept right to privacy is a wide-ranging term, which cannot be defined exhaustively, but includes, among other-protected forums, sexual life, and the right to establish and develop relationships with other human beings'.[46]

In its definition and scope of the right to privacy, the IACtHR constantly mentions and refers to in its rulings some decisions of the European Court of Human

41. *Ibid.*, para. 194. This jurisprudence has been restated by the Court in other cases, such as: Case of *Escué-Zapata v. Colombia*, Judgment of 4 Jul. 2007 (Merits, Reparations and Costs), para. 95; Case of *Tristán Donoso v. Panama*, Judgment of 27 Jan. 2009, para. 55; *Escher et al. v. Brazil*, Judgment of 6 Jul. 2009, para. 113; and Case *Fernández Prieto and Tumbeiro v. Argentina*, Judgment of 1 Sep. 2020, para. 102.
42. Cfr. Inter-American Court of Human Rights. Case of *Tristán Donoso v. Panama*, Judgment of 27 Jan. 2009, para. 55. Available at: https://www.corteidh.or.cr/docs/casos/articulos/seriec_193_ing.pdf.
43. Inter-American Court of Human Rights. Case of *Escher et al. v. Brazil*, Judgment of 6 Jul. 2009, para. 114. Available at: https://www.corteidh.or.cr/docs/casos/articulos/seriec_200_ing.pdf.
44. *Ibid.*, para. 115.
45. Inter-American Court of Human Rights. Case of *Tristán Donoso v. Panama*, Judgment of 27 Jan. 2009, para. 56. This criterion can also be found in the case of *Escher et al. v. Brazil*, Judgment of 6 Jul. 2009, para. 116.
46. Inter-American Court of Human Rights. Case of *Fernández Ortega et al. v. Mexico*, Judgment of 30 Aug. 2010, para. 129; and Case of *Rosendo Cantú v. Mexico*, Judgment of 31 Aug. 2010, para. 119.

Rights regarding Article 8 of the European Convention on Human Rights as reference. The evolution of the right to privacy in the Inter-American human rights system has a strong influence on the European system, and in both, this fundamental right has gradually been expanded.[47]

In its most recent judgment concerning Article 11 of the ACHR, the IACtHR has associated the right to privacy with the right to informed consent in terms of health. In this regard, the IACtHR has resolved that 'the violation of the right to informed consent implies not only a violation of the right to health, but also the right to personal freedom, the right to dignity and private life, and the right to access to information'.[48]

In other resolutions, the IACtHR has noted that the right to private life is not limited to right to privacy, as it encompasses a series of factors related to dignity, including, for example, the ability to develop one's own personality and aspirations, develop one's own identity and personal relationships with other human beings and with the outside world, as well as the right to personal autonomy.[49]

§3. Updated Principles on Privacy and Personal Data Protection Approved by the CJI

58. On 9 April 2021, the Inter-American Juridical Committee (CJI), a consultative body of the OAS, approved in its ninety-eighth Regular Session the 'Updated Principles on Privacy and the Personal Data Protection, with Annotations'.[50]

59. This document consists of two sections: (1) the first includes the thirteen principles of the right to personal data protection and (2) the second one provides 'annotations on each of them and specific recommendations for their implementations'.

60. The principles included in the first section of the document are the following: (1) Lawful Purposes and Loyalty; (2) Transparency and Consent; (3) Relevance and Necessity; (4) Limited Processing and Retention; (5) Confidentiality; (6) Security of Data; (7) Accuracy of Data; (8) Access, Rectification, Erasure, Objection and Portability; (9) Sensitive Personal Data; (10) Accountability; (11) Transborder Flow of Data and Accountability; (12) Exceptions; and (13) Data Protection Authorities.

---

47. This influence can be observed since the case of the *Ituango Massacres v. Colombia*, Judgment of 1 Jul. 2006 (Preliminary Objections, Merits, Reparations and Costs), para. 195.
48. Inter-American Court of Human Rights. Case of *Guachalá Chimbo et al. v. Ecuador*, Judgment of 26 Mar. 2021, para. 110. [authors translation] Available at: https://www.corteidh.or.cr/docs/casos/articulos/seriec_423_esp.pdf.
49. Cfr. Inter-American Court of Human Rights. Case of *López et al. v. Argentina*, Judgment of 25 Nov. 2019, para. 97; Case of *I.V. v. Bolivia*, Judgment of 30 Nov. 2016, para. 122; Case of *Artavia Murillo et al. v. Costa Rica*, Judgment of 28 Nov. 2012, para. 143, among others.
50. The 'Updated Principles on Privacy and the Personal Data Protection, with Annotations' are available at: http://www.oas.org/en/sla/iajc/docs/CJI-doc_638-21_EN.pdf.

61. The Updated Principles reinforce the principles of transparency, accountability of controllers and data processors, as well as the security of personal data and the empowerment of data subjects by recognizing the rights of erasure and portability. This update effort is consistent with the global need to adapt the privacy and personal data protection regulatory framework pursuant to technological changes and the digital environment. Additionally, like all the international instruments related to this topic, the Updated Principles include provisions to harmonized privacy and personal data protection with transborder data flows to guarantee economic development.

62. It should be noted that currently the OECD has thirty-eight members, including Mexico, Chile, Colombia and recently Costa Rica. Mexico's accession to the OECD was in 1994.[51]

§4. Commercial Treaties

I. World Trade Organization

63. Mexico is a member of the WTO since 1 January 1995 and a member of GATT since 24 August 1986.[52] Article XIV section (c)(ii) of the GATS[53] provides the commercial legal framework for WTO Members to take necessary measures to secure compliance with laws or regulations which are not inconsistent with the provisions of this Agreement, including those relating to the protection of privacy of individuals in relation to the processing and dissemination of personal data and the protection of confidentiality of individual records and accounts.

Under this provision, WTO Member States should take the necessary steps and freely adapt their respective privacy laws and practices for the protection of the privacy of individuals, including the collection, processing and disclosure of personal data, and the protection of confidentiality of individual records and accounts. Likewise, under this provision, WTO Members are expected to enact consistent legal frameworks concerning the protection of data and information of individuals when entering into commercial treaties with other regional blocks or third countries.

II. US-Mexico-Canada Trade Agreement (USMCA)

64. Chapter 19 of the USMCA contains Article (19.8) on Personal Information Protection which recognizes the economic and social benefits of protecting the

51. The list of the member countries of the OECD is available at: https://www.oecd.org/about/members-and-partners/.
52. The section on Mexico of the WTO is available at: https://www.wto.org/english/thewto_e/countries_e/mexico_e.htm.
53. The GATS consist of a set of multilateral rules covering trade and services, which operates under the umbrella of WTO. The GATS has been in force since January 1995. *See:* Understanding the WTO: The Agreements at: https://www.wto.org/english/thewto_e/whatis_e/tif_e/agrm6_e.htm.

personal information of users of digital trade and the contribution that this makes to enhancing consumer confidence in digital trade.[54]

Section 2 of Article 19.8 establishes that each party shall adopt or maintain a legal framework that provides for the protection of the personal information of the users of digital trade. In the development of its legal framework for the protection of personal information, each party should take into account principles and guidelines of relevant international bodies, such as the *APEC Privacy Framework* and the *OECD Recommendation of the Council concerning Guidelines governing the protection of Privacy and Transborder Flows of Personal Data (2013).*

Section 3 provides that the parties recognize that these key principles include: limitation on collection, choice, data quality, purpose specification, use limitation, security safeguards, transparency, individual participation and accountability. The parties also recognize the importance of ensuring compliance with measures to protect personal information and ensuring that any restrictions on cross-border flows of personal information are necessary and proportionate to the risks presented.

Section 4 establishes that each party shall endeavour to adopt non-discriminatory practices in protecting users of digital trade from personal information protection violations occurring within its jurisdiction.

Section 5 provides that each party shall publish information on the personal information protections it provides to users of digital trade, including how: (a) individual can pursue remedies; and (b) business can comply with any legal requirements.

Section 6 recognizes that the parties may take different legal approaches to protection of personal information, and that each party should encourage the development of mechanism to promote compatibility between these different regimes. The parties shall endeavour to exchange information on the mechanisms applied in their jurisdiction and explore ways to extend these or other suitable arrangements to promote compatibility between them. The parties recognize that the *APEC Cross-Border Privacy Rules* system is a valid mechanism to facilitate cross-border information transfers while protecting personal information.

65. Likewise, Article 19.11 of the USMCA establishes prohibitions and restrictions on the cross-border transfer of information, including personal information, by electronic means if this activity is for the conduct of the business of a covered person.

Section 2 of Article 19.11 establishes that nothing in this article shall prevent a party from adopting or maintaining a measure inconsistent with paragraph 1 necessary to achieve a legitimate public policy objective, provided that the measure: (a) is not applied in a manner which would constitute a means of arbitrary or unjustifiable discrimination or a disguised restriction on trade; or (b) does not impose restrictions on transfers of information greater than are necessary to achieve the objective.

---

54. Chapter 19 on Digital Trade of the USMCA is available at: https://ustr.gov/sites/default/files/files/agreements/FTA/USMCA/Text/19-Digital-Trade.pdf.

III. The EU–Mexico Trade Agreement

66. The European Union and Mexico are linked by a system of agreements, covering the whole of the political, economic and trade relationship. The basis of this relationship is the *Economic Partnership, Political Coordination and Cooperation Agreement Between the European Community and Its Member States, of the One Part, and the United Mexican States, of the Other Part* (hereinafter referred to as the EU–Mexico Agreement).[55] The *EU–Mexico Agreement* covers broad issues that go far beyond trade, including political issues, climate change and human rights. The *EU–Mexico Agreement* was adopted by the EU Council on 28 September 2000 after the notification by the contracting parties of the completion of the procedures necessary for entry into force. The *EU–Mexico Agreement* entered into force on 1 October 2000.

67. Article 20 section(g) of the EU–Mexico Agreement, which specifically deals with information society issues, provides that the parties shall particularly cooperate on a dialogue on regulatory cooperation concerning international online services, including aspects related to the protection of privacy and personal data.

Article 39.2(c) deals with the cooperation on human rights and democracy, and establishes that the parties agree to cooperate mainly in the promotion of human rights and democratic principles.

68. Some of the most relevant provisions of *the EU–Mexico Agreement* are Articles 41 and 51, dealing with cooperation on data protection. Pursuant to Article 41 of *the EU–Mexico Agreement*, Mexico agreed to cooperate with the EU on the protection of personal data in order to improve the level of protection and avoid obstacles to trade that requires transfers of personal data. Cooperation on personal data protection may include technical assistance in the form of exchange of information and experts and the establishment of joint programmes and projects.

69. Under Article 51, Mexico and the EU agreed to accord a high level of protection to the processing of personal data in accordance with the standards adopted by the relevant international organizations. Article 51 textually provides:

> Data protection
>
> 1. The Parties agree to accord a high level of protection to the processing of personal and other data, in accordance with the standards adopted by the relevant international organizations and the Community.

55. The *EU–Mexico Trade Agreement* is primarily based on three pillars: (i) political dialogue; (ii) trade liberalization; and (iii) cooperation. A Joint Ministerial Council is in charge of the implementation and oversight of this agreement. The official documents containing the background of the negotiations, the full text of the treaty, the information concerning the entry into force and the documents relating to meetings and decisions of the EU–Mexico Joint Council, additional protocols and joint declarations are available in the website of SICE at: http://www.sice.oas.org/TPD/MEX_EU/MEX_EU_e.ASP.

2. To this end they shall take account of the standards referred to in the Annex which shall form an integral part of this Agreement.

The standards referred to in such Annex are: (i) guidelines for the regulation of computerized personal data files, modified by the General Assembly of the United Nations on 20 November 1990; (ii) recommendation of the OECD Council concerning guidelines governing the protection of privacy and transborder flows of personal data of 23 September 1980; (iii) CoE Convention 108 of 28 January 1981; and (iv) Directive 95/46/EC of the European Parliament and of the Council of 24 October 1995 on the protection of individuals with regard to the processing of personal data and on the free movement of such data, the latter has been repealed by the GDPR.

70. The framework for privacy and data protection under *the EU–Mexico Agreement* is fairly broad, and its focus is mainly on the promotion and protection of human rights and data protection cooperation. Mexico and the EU have agreed to provide a high level of protection to the processing of personal data pursuant to relevant standards adopted by international organizations and the EU entities.

The EU and Mexico launched in May 2016 negotiations to modernize the *EU–Mexico Agreement.* The latest round of negotiations took place in Mexico City in January 2018, and the consolidated text was last amended and modernized on 1 March 2020. The modernization of the *EU–Mexico Agreement* did not include any new proposals to reform aspects concerning privacy and data protection covered under Articles 41 and 51.

IV. Comprehensive and Progressive Agreement for Trans-Pacific Partnership

71. The Comprehensive and Progressive Agreement for Trans-Pacific Partnership (hereinafter CPTPP), signed on 8 March 2018 in Santiago de Chile, is a free trade agreement between Australia, Brunei Darussalam, Canada, Chile, Japan, Malaysia, Mexico, Peru, New Zealand, Singapore and Vietnam. The immediate precedent for this agreement was the TPP Agreement, signed by the Ministers of said countries on 4 February 2016 in Auckland, New Zealand. After the withdrawal of the United States in 2017, the remaining parties negotiated this new version of the agreement, and it entered into force on 30 December 2018 for Mexico. The CPTPP incorporates most of the provisions of the TPP, with the exception of a limited set of suspended provisions.

72. Chapter 14 of the CPTPP contains Article 14.8 on Personal Information Protection which recognizes 'the economic and social benefits of protecting the personal information of users of electronic commerce and the contribution that this makes to enhancing consumer confidence in electronic commerce'. This provision places an obligation on parties to adopt or maintain a legal framework that provides for the protection of personal information of the users of electronic commerce. It does not introduce explicit measures about how to provide for the protection of personal information, but it establishes that parties shall consider the principles and guidelines of relevant international bodies and publish information, including how individuals can pursue remedies, as well as how businesses can comply with legal requirements.

73. Article 14.11 of the CPTPP enhances cross-border transfer of information by electronic means, including personal information, without any specific provisions on how to protect it. Instead, said provision stipulates that each party may have its own regulatory requirements concerning the transfer of information.

V. APEC Cross-Border Privacy Rules

74. Mexico endorsed the *APEC Privacy Framework* in 2005 and its updated version of 2015.[56] As a result of the needs to transfer personal information across the twenty-one members of the Asia-Pacific region, APEC developed in 2011 a system of rules to facilitate the transfers of personal data between member economies of the APEC, known as the Cross Border Privacy Rules (CBPR).[57] Unlike the data protection rules contained in the USMCA and the EU-Mexico Trade Agreement, the CBPR rules are non-binding, and they are only applicable to APEC member economies that have voluntarily decided to endorse them.

The CBPR is a mechanism for compliance with the APEC privacy principles to transfer personal data across borders, but it does not replace national and domestic laws or other data protection standards or commitments that a country might have previously endorsed or ratified including international treaties.[58] Currently, only nine countries are participating in the APEC's CBPR system.[59]

75. Mexico endorsed the CBPR in January 2013.[60] However, the National Institute for Transparency, Access to Information and Personal Data Protection (INAI) has not yet fully implemented the criteria concerning the eligibility to select accountability agents that will be responsible for issuing the certifications to interested parties, as well as the coordination with the data protection agencies of participating economies in the APEC CBPR System. In other words, the CBPR are not

56. APEC Privacy Framework is available at: https://www.apec.org/Publications/2005/12/APEC-Privacy-Framework.
57. APEC's CBPR is a government-backed data privacy certification that companies can join to demonstrate compliance with internationally recognized data privacy protection in the context of international trade, *see* APEC, 'What is the Cross-Border Privacy Rules System' https://www.apec.org/About-Us/About-APEC/Fact-Sheets/What-is-the-Cross-Border-Privacy-Rules-System.
58. For an overview on how the CBPR works and the major differences with the GDPR, *see* Gribakov, Andrei, *'Cross-Border Privacy Rules in Asia: An Overview'*, Lawfare blog, 3 Jan. 2019, available at: https://www.lawfareblog.com/cross-border-privacy-rules-asia-overview.
59. *See* the website of the CBPR at: http://cbprs.org/.
60. Global Tax News, 'Mexico participates in APEC Cross-Border Privacy System', 17 Jan. 2013, available at: https://bit.ly/3tNXfF8.

yet fully operative in Mexico, and this is still a pending task that remains to be coordinated between the SE and the INAI in order to implement the commitments of Mexico under APEC.

The Membership of Mexico in Multilateral and Regional Organizations related to Privacy and Data Protection is compiled and resumed in Table 1.

Table 1 Membership of Mexico in Multilateral and Regional Organizations Related to Privacy and Data Protection

Name of Organization	*Name of Group or Committee*	*Participant Government Agency and Unit*	*Policy Area*	*Website*
1. OECD	Committee on Digital Economy Policy. Working Party on Data Governance and Privacy	– SE. – Instituto Nacional de Transparencia, Acceso a la Información y Protección de Datos Personales (INAI).	Data Privacy, Data Governance, Cross-Border Data Flows.	https://bit.ly/3qlT2qc
2. Global Privacy Assembly (GPA)	Mexico is part of the Assembly and participates actively in the meetings of the GPA.	– INAI. – INFOCDMX. – Instituto de Transparencia, Acceso a la Información Pública y Protección de Datos Personales del Estado de México y Municipios (INFOEM).	Data Privacy, Data Governance, Cross-Border Data Flows.	https://bit.ly/3am1Y9h
3. CoE	Consultative Committee of Convention 108 (T-PD) Mexico has observatory status.	– INAI.	Human Rights Data Privacy, Cross-Border Data Flows.	https://bit.ly/3u1vLMb

Name of Organization	*Name of Group or Committee*	*Participant Government Agency and Unit*	*Policy Area*	*Website*
4. APEC	Digital Economy Steering Group.	– SE	E-Commerce Data Privacy, Security, Cross-Border Data Flows.	https://bit.ly/2N07vty
5. RIPD	Executive Committee of the RIPD.	– INAI. – INFOCDMX. – INFOEM.	Privacy, Data Protection, Cross-Border Transfers.	https://bit.ly/2N95E5p

Source: Own with *information* contained in websites.

Chapter 3. Privacy in Electronic Communications (Including Rules Regarding Use of Cookies, Etc.)

76. Unlike the EU, Mexico does not have a special regulation like the *e-Privacy Directive* (currently the Proposal of the EC Regulation on Privacy and Electronic Communications)[61] that governs privacy and processing of personal data for the electronic communication sectors. In Mexico, the rules on privacy for the telecommunication sector are contained in Article 145 section III of the Federal Law of Telecommunications and Broadcasting.[62] That section establishes that the concessionaires and authorized entities that render the service of access to Internet shall preserve the privacy of users and the security of the network. Since communication service providers and telcos are private entities, they are specifically governed and covered by the rules contained in the Federal Law on Protection of Personal Data Held by Private Parties (FLPPDPP) and its Regulation (RFLPPDPP).

The FLPPDPP and its Regulation are of general observance in the Mexican Republic, and their main purpose is to protect personal data in possession of private sector entities with the aim to ensure the privacy of individuals and their right to informational self-determination.

More detailed information about the FLPPDPP and its Regulation is analysed in Part II of this monograph.

Regulation of Cookies

77. INAI has issued a set of guidelines to provide for a better understanding and interpretation of the provisions of the FLPPDPP and its Regulation. On 17 January 2013, the SE issued *Privacy Notice Guidelines* which were drafted in cooperation with the national data protection agency INAI.[63] The *Privacy Notice Guidelines* set forth opt-out requirements for the use of cookies, web beacons and similar technologies. These guidelines include specific requirements on the content and delivery of privacy notices generally.

78. Under the *Privacy Notice Guidelines*, if a data controller uses mechanisms such as cookies or web beacons to collect personal data while a user interacts with the mechanism, the controller must provide the user with a '*communication or announcement located in a visible place*' and information on how to deactivate the collection of the data. The communication or announcement must be provided at the moment the user interacts with the mechanism (for instance, when the user visits the website or downloads the app), and it must take place outside the privacy notice. Separately, these guidelines establish that the privacy notice must contain detailed

---

61. The Proposal of the EC Regulation on Privacy and Electronic Communications is available at: https://eur-lex.europa.eu/legal-content/EN/TXT/?uri=CELEX%3A52017PC0010.
62. The FLTB is available at: http://www.diputados.gob.mx/LeyesBiblio/pdf/LFTR_110121.pdf.
63. The Privacy Notice Guidelines (Lineamientos del Aviso de Privacidad) were published in DOF on 17 Jan. 2013, available at: http://www.dof.gob.mx/nota_detalle.php?codigo=5284966&fecha=17/01/2013.

and sufficient information about the data controller's practices with respect to the personal information collected through the use of this technology.

79. Although there is not any express infringement regulated in the FLPPDPP and its Regulation concerning the use of cookies, their use in contravention of the *Privacy Notice Guidelines* may result in the infringement of the principle of unlawful collection of personal information, which could be sanctioned with a fine from 100 to 160,000 minimum salary days (EUR 492–EUR 786,000 approx.) and if the infringement persists, an additional fine of up to from 100 to 320,000 minimum salary days (EUR 492–EUR 1,572,000 approx.) may be imposed.

Chapter 4. Other Relevant National Legal Provisions Regarding the Protection of Privacy (Not In-Depth Analysis but Overview; In-Depth Analysis in Part X)

80. Mexico has more than forty-four federal laws that regulate aspects concerning privacy, the confidentiality of information and records, as well as the collection and processing of personal information in different areas that are compiled and resumed in Table 2.[64]

81. In the context of electronic commerce, the Federal Consumer Protection Law (FCPL) contains a list of obligations for suppliers' and consumers' rights for online transactions.

Under Article 76*bis* of the FCPL, suppliers have the following obligations concerning the use of the information of consumers:

(i) Use the information provided by the consumer in a confidential manner, and not disclose or transmit it to other providers, unless the consumer has provided a written authorization or has been requested by a competent authority.
(ii) Make use of available technical elements in order to provide security and confidentiality to the information provided to the consumer and to inform the consumer prior to the conclusion of a transaction about the general characteristics of such technical elements.
(iii) Disclose consumers the following data before entering into a transaction: address, phone number and other data where the consumer could be heard, file his claims or request explanations.
(iv) Respect the decision of the consumer concerning the quantity and quality of the products he wishes to receive as well as that of not receiving unsolicited commercial mails.
(v) Abstain from using, selling or advertising strategies that do not provide clear and sufficient information on the services offered to the consumer, particularly marketing practices directed to vulnerable people, such as children, the elderly and sick, incorporating mechanisms that warn when the information will not be apt for a vulnerable sector of the population.

82. Mexico enacted a comprehensive federal law in January 2017, the GLPPDPGPSI. This law specifically regulates the collection, use and processing of personal information exclusively in possession of government and public sector entities. The *GLPPDPGPSI* governs public entities of the federal, state and municipal level, as well as any authority, entity, agency or organization of the Executive,

64. Please note that Table 2 is not exhaustive, since there may be other future laws and regulations at the federal level with provisions concerning confidentiality of information and records and the protection of privacy.

Legislative and Judicial branches, autonomous bodies, political parties, trusts and public funds.[65]

65. The General Law on Protection of Personal Data in Possession of Government and Public Sector Institutions (GLPPDPGPSI) published in DOF of 26 Jan. 2017 is available at: http://www.dof.gob.mx/nota_detalle.php?codigo=5469949&fecha=26/01/2017.

Table 2 Federal Laws in Mexico with Provisions on Confidentiality, Privacy and Personal Data Protection

Title of the Law	*Provision Number(s)*	*Enforcement Authorities*	*Scope of the Provision(s)*
1. Federal Civil Code (*Código Civil Federal*)	Articles 58–60, 134, 1916	Federal Civil Courts (*Juzgados en Materia Civil Federal*)	Data requirements that national birth certificates should contain. Requirements for the rectification or modification requests of a certificate on civil status before the Federal Judicial Power. Regulates moral damage consisting of an injury suffered by an individual in his private life.
2. Law for the Regulation of Article 5 of the Federal Constitution Pertaining to the Practice of Professions in the Federal District (Ley Reglamentaria del Artículo 5o. Constitucional Relativa al Ejercicio de Profesiones en la Ciudad de Mexico)	Article 36	Ministry of Public Education (*Secretaría de Educación Pública*)	Obligation of professionals to keep the confidentiality and secrecy of matters entrusted by their clients.
3. Law of the Professional Carrier Service in the Federal Public Administration (*Ley del Servicio Profesional de Carrera en la Administración Pública Federal*)	Article 15	Ministry of Public Administration and the Federal Judicial Power (*SFP y el Poder Judicial Federal*)	Confidentiality of the data contained in the Sole Registry of the Public Professional Service

Title of the Law	*Provision Number(s)*	*Enforcement Authorities*	*Scope of the Provision(s)*
4. General Law of Administrative Responsibilities (*Ley General de Responsabilidades Administrativas*)	Article 34, Article 28, Article 29, Article 95, Article 55, Article 56, and Article 49 section V	Ministry of Public Administration and the Federal Judicial Power (*SFP y el Poder Judicial Federal*)	Obligation of public servants to guard and look after the documentation and information under their responsibility, faculty of Public Ministry, the courts, or the judicial authorities to use information related to the declarations of patrimonial situation and when the investigating, substantiating, or resolving authorities require it duo to an investigation or resolution of administrative responsibilities. Obligation of the investigating authorities to keep the information confidential or secrecy. Liability for using privileged information for personal interests.
5. Federal Law of Administrative Procedure (*Ley Federal del Procedimiento Administrativo*)	Article 33	Entities of the Federal Public Administration	Right to access to information and documents from the corresponding administrative offices, except for information pertaining to defence and national security in matters protected by the commercial or industrial secret where the data subject may not be a party.

Title of the Law	*Provision Number(s)*	*Enforcement Authorities*	*Scope of the Provision(s)*
6. Federal Consumer Protection Law (*Ley Federal de Protección al Consumidor*)	Articles 1, 16, 17, 18, 18*bis*, 76*bis* and section VIII	Office of the Federal Attorney for Consumer Protection (*Profeco*)	Confidentiality and protection of consumer information for marketing and advertising purposes. Consumer opt-out from advertisement and prohibition to transfer information to third parties. Security safeguards for consumer information.
7. Code of Commerce (*Código de Comercio*)	Article 49	Ministry of Economy and Mercantile Tribunals (*SE y Juzgados Mercantiles)*	Preservation of documents contained in data messages for the term of ten years.
8. Federal Law of Economic Competition *(Ley Federal de Competencia Económica)*	*Article 3 section IX-XI, Article 14 section VII, Article 17, Article 23 section V, Article 35, Article 49, Article 76, Article 105 section VI, Article 124, Article 125*	Federal Competition Comisión and the Ministry of Economics *(COFECE y SE)*	Confidentiality of the information obtained by the FCC during search and investigation procedures. Liability of public servants in case of disclosure of information and security safeguards. Criteria for the classification of reserved, confidential and public information.
9. Federal Law of Authors Right (*Ley Federal del Derecho de Autor*)	Articles 109 and 231	The National Institute for Copyright and Federal Criminal Courts*(Instituto Nacional del Derecho de Autor y Juzgados Penales Federales*)	Obligation to obtain prior authorization to access, reproduce, distribute and disclose individual's information contained in databases and prohibition to distribute copyright-protected works without the authorization of the corresponding holder.

Title of the Law	*Provision Number(s)*	*Enforcement Authorities*	*Scope of the Provision(s)*
10. Federal Law for the Protection of Industrial Property (*Ley Federal de Protección a la Propiedad Industrial*)	Articles 2, 23, 163-169, Article 334, Article 386 section XIV, 402 section V	The Mexican Institute of Industrial Property and Federal Criminal Courts (*IMPI y Juzgados Penales Federales*)	Confidentiality of industrial secrets and conditions to disclose them to third parties, and liability of public officials.
11. The Law for the Protection and Defence of the User of Financial Services (*Ley de Protección y Defensa Al Usuario de Servicios Financieros*)	Articles 13–15	National Commission for the Protection and Defence of Users of Financial Services (*Condusef*)	Obligation to keep reserve and confidentiality on documents, deposits and transactions carried out by financial institutions and liability of public officials as a result of the breach of the banking, fiduciary or secret securities.
12. Law of Credit Institutions (*Ley de Instituciones de Crédito*)	Article 10 section IV, Article 46*bis* 1 section I, 93 section II, 97 section III, Article 101*bis* IV, Article 112*bis* section III, V and VI, Article 112*Quáter*, Article 115, Article 124, 142 section IX, 143, 185, 194 section VIII	The Banking and Securities National Commission and Federal Criminal Courts (*CNBVs y Juzgados Penales Federales*)	Confidentiality of clients' documents and prohibition to disclose news or information on deposits, transactions or services. Exemptions and conditions to disclose information to public authorities and officials. Liability of public officials as a result of the breach of the banking, fiduciary or securities secret. Access to information request conditions. Conditions to disclose foreign financial authorities' information on the transactions and services from credit institutions.

Title of the Law	*Provision Number(s)*	*Enforcement Authorities*	*Scope of the Provision(s)*
13. Securities Market Law (*Ley del Mercado de Valores*)	Article 36 section I, Article 345, Article 358, Article 364 section II, Articles 380 and 381	The Banking and Securities National Commission and Federal Criminal Courts (*CNBV y Juzgados Penales Federales*)	Prohibition to Stock Exchanges to disclose news or information on transactions and services where they participate. Liability of Directors and employees of Stock Exchanges as a result of the breach of the securities secret. Conditions to disclose foreign financial authorities' information on the transactions registered by securities exchanges.
14. Saving and Popular Credit Law (*Ley de Ahorro y Crédito Popular*)	Article 34	The Banking and Securities National Commission and Federal Criminal Courts (*CNBV y Juzgados Penales Federales*)	Prohibition to Entities to disclose news or information on the deposits, services or transactions.
15. Investment Funds Law (Ley de Fondos de Inversión)	Article 55	The Banking and Securities National Commission and Federal Criminal Courts (*CNBV y Juzgados Penales Federales*)	Prohibition to Investment Partnerships to disclose news or information on transactions and services where they participate. Liability of Directors and employees of Investment Partnerships as a result of the breach of the investment secret. Conditions to disclose foreign financial authorities' information on the transactions registered by Investment Partnerships and the persons rendering services.

Title of the Law	*Provision Number(s)*	*Enforcement Authorities*	*Scope of the Provision(s)*
16. Law to Regulate Credit Information Partnerships (*Ley para Regular las Sociedades de Información Crediticia*)	Articles 18, 28, 37, 38, 39, 52 and section I	The Banking and Securities National Commission and Federal Criminal Courts (*CNBV y Juzgados Penales Federales*)	Prohibition to Credit Information Partnerships to request and disclose information. Terms and conditions to provide information authorizations on credit reports to users. Liability of partnerships' employees as a result of disclosure of the financial secret. Security safeguards obligations for partnerships.
17. Law of the Bank of Mexico (*Ley del Banco de México*)	Article 58	The Bank of Mexico trough the Governor and the Members of the Government Board (*Banxico a través del Gobernador y la Junta de Gobierno*)	Obligation of the members of the Government Junta, civil servants and employees to preserve the banking and fiduciary secrets provided in financial and banking laws.
18. Fiscal Code of the Federation (*Código Fiscal de la Federación*)	Articles 17-D, 17-J, 69	The Federal Tax Administration and Federal Criminal Courts (*Secretaría de Hacienda y Crédito Público y Juzgados Penales Federales*)	Data obtained from taxpayers form part of the integrated system of the population registry provided in the General Law of Population and its Regulation. Revocation of an electronic certificate as a result of a breach of a person's privacy during an e-signature creation. Obligations of public officials to keep the confidentiality and reserve of statements and data provided by tax contributors. Conditions to

Title of the Law	*Provision Number(s)*	*Enforcement Authorities*	*Scope of the Provision(s)*
			disclose information to foreign fiscal authorities.
19. *Law of the National system of Statistical and Geographic Information* (Ley del Sistema Nacional de Información Estadística y Geografía)	Articles 37-47 and Article 73, section V	The National Institute on Statistics, Geography and Informatics and the Federal Criminal Courts (*INEGI y Juzgados Penales Federales*)	Protection of the reserve and confidentiality of individuals' data for geographical, statistical and census purposes. Conditions and terms to request modifications of personal data. Obligations to capture produce, process and disclose information for the integration of the national census system.
20. General Law of Population (*Ley General de Población*)	Articles 91, 98, 101, 103–105, 107, 112, 113 section I	The State Department and Federal Criminal Courts (*Secretaría de Gobernación y Juzgados Penales Federales*)	Identity and registry of individuals in the National Registry of Population. Obligation of Mexican citizens to register in the National Citizenship Registry and obtain their Citizen Identity identification as an official means of identification in Mexico and abroad. Data verification of the State Department regarding the identity of Mexican citizens and obligations of government entities to disclose information requested by the State Department. Obligations of the State Department to provide the IFE information pertaining to the National Citizenship Registry.

Title of the Law	*Provision Number(s)*	*Enforcement Authorities*	*Scope of the Provision(s)*
			Penalties and removal of employees of the State Department when they disclose confidential information without being authorized to do so.
21. Federal Labour Law (*Ley Federal del Trabajo*)	Article 47 section IX, Article 134 section XIII Federal Labour Tribunals on Conciliation and Arbitration (*Juntas Federales de Conciliación y Arbitraje*)	The law provides for the termination of a labour agreement without liability of the employer, when the worker discloses manufacturing secrets or matters of reserved character in detriment of the company. Obligation of the workers to scrupulously keep technical, commercial and manufacturing secrets of those products in which they are directly or indirectly involved or of those they have knowledge of, as a result of the work they develop, as well as reserved administrative matters where its disclosure may damage a company.	
22. General Law of Electoral Institutions and Procedures (*Ley General de Instituciones y Procedimientos Electorales*)	Article 39 section 2, Article 117 section g, Article 148, Article 491, Article 126 section 4, Article 217 section g, Article 336 section 3, Article 491	The INE and Federal Criminal Courts (*Instituto Federal Electoral y Juzgados Penales Federales*)	Confidentiality of documents, data and information provided by citizens to the Federal Electoral Registry and disclosure conditions. Conditions for government entities to have access to information conforming the electoral census registry. Data

Title of the Law	*Provision Number(s)*	*Enforcement Authorities*	*Scope of the Provision(s)*
			information that the Mexican General Catalogue of Electors should contain.
23. Law of Audit and Accountability of the Federation (*Ley de Fiscalización y Rendición de Cuentas de la Federación*)	Articles 89 subsection XXVIII, 17 subsection XI and 92 subsection III.	Federal Superior Auditor and Chamber of Deputies (Auditoría Superior de la Federación y Cámara de Diputados del Congreso de la Unión).	Obligations for the Federal Superior Auditor to keep the confidentiality of information and documents. Criminal liability for disclosure of reserved and confidential information.
24. Federal Law of Public Commission (*Ley de Correduría Pública*)	Article 15 section V	Ministry of Economy and the Federal Criminal Courts (*SE y los Juzgados Penales Federales*)	Obligation of the *Corredor Público* to keep professional secrets pertaining his activities, and prohibition to disclose names, data and information of contracting parties in juridical acts unless it is required by the nature of the transaction or through the consent of the parties.
25. Federal Criminal Code (*Código Penal Federal*)	Articles 173, 177, 210, 211, 211*bis* 1–7	Federal Criminal Courts (*Juzgados Penales Federales*)	Labour journeys in favour of the community to those who unduly open or intercept written communications. Imprisonment and penalties to those who intercept private communications without a judicial order. Imprisonment and penalties for disclosing secret or reserved communication known or received

Title of the Law	*Provision Number(s)*	*Enforcement Authorities*	*Scope of the Provision(s)*
			by virtue of employment or occupation. Liability for professionals, public servants, state employees and functionaries of financial institutions as a result of disclosure of information, images during an intervention of a private communication. Imprisonment and penalties for modifying, destroying, obtaining access or copying and causing loss of information contained in computer systems or computer equipment protected by security measures.
26. Law on Crimes of the Press (*Ley Sobre Delitos de Imprenta*)	Articles 2–3, 9–12	The Federal Judicial Power (*Poder Judicial Federal*)	Legal hypothesis of attacks on the private life, the morals and the public peace and crimes related to hate and malicious expression and speech. The prohibition to publish personal data without the consent of the interested parties in documents related to criminal procedures, family law matters, secret commission of the army and issues pertaining to military operations and victims of crime. Fines, imprisonment punishments and removal of public servants and state employees.

Title of the Law	*Provision Number(s)*	*Enforcement Authorities*	*Scope of the Provision(s)*
27. Federal Law Against Organized Crime (*Ley Federal Contra la Delincuencia Organizada*)	Articles 16–21, Articles 24, 26, 27 and 28	The Federal Judicial Power (*Poder Judicial Federal*)	Legal hypothesis and modalities to authorize the interception of private communications by judicial authorities. Obligations to keep the reserve of the content of an intervention of private communications. Fines and imprisonment punishments to public officials, employees and individuals that disclose and use information or images of a person in the course of intervention of private communications.
28. National Security Law (*Ley de Seguridad Nacional*)	Articles 6, 10, 53, 59, 64	The Federal Judicial Power (*Poder Judicial Federal*)	Obligations of preservation and confidentiality of information for national security entities and its contractors. Confidentiality obligations for public servants or individuals who are granted access to information pertaining to national security. Obligations to protect the privacy and dignity of individuals, and the reserve of the information contained in official reports and documents.

Title of the Law	*Provision Number(s)*	*Enforcement Authorities*	*Scope of the Provision(s)*
29. Federal Law on Protection of Personal Data Held by Private Parties (*Ley Federal de Protección de Datos en Posesión de los Particulares*)	Articles 1–69	The National Institute of Access to Information and Data Protection and the Ministry of Economics (*INAI and SE*)	Obligations for companies and data processors to protect personal information of individuals and to provide mechanisms for the exercise of the rights of access, rectification, cancellation and opposition.
30. Federal Law of Telecommunications and Broadcasting (*Ley Federal de Telecommunicaciones y Radiodifusión*)	Article 145 subsection III, 298 D) V	Federal Telecommunications Institute (*IFT*)	Obligations for telecommunications. Concessionaires to maintain. The privacy and security of users in the network. Fines for not establishing measures to protect the privacy and confidentiality of the communication of users.
31. National Code of Criminal Procedure (*Código Nacional de Procedimientos Penales)*	Articles 15 and 50	The Federal Judicial Power (*Poder Judicial Federal*)	Obligation to protect the private sphere and personal data of any party involved in a criminal procedure pursuant to the Constitution and applicable legislation. Protection of privacy in facilitating access to digital files in criminal proceedings.

Title of the Law	*Provision Number(s)*	*Enforcement Authorities*	*Scope of the Provision(s)*
32. Advanced Electronic Signature Law (*Ley de Firma Electrónica Avanzada*)	Articles 14 and 25 subsection VI	Ministry of Public Function, the Ministry of Economy and other administrative authorities (*Secretaría de la Función Pública, Secretaría de Economía y otras autoridades administrativas*)	Obligation to preserve the confidentiality, integrity and security of personal data of the holders of digital certificates.
33. General Archives Law (*Ley General de Archivos*)	Articles 6, 11 *in fine*, 36, 37, 38, 60, 61, 62	General National Archive, Ministry of Public Function and the Federal Judicial Power (*Archivo General de la Nación, Secretaría de la Función Pública y Poder Judicial Federal*)	Provisions to ensure the preservation, integrity, availability, accessibility and confidentiality of the information contained in documentary archives. It establishes some provisions with respect to personal data, sensitive personal data and the retention periods. It also includes rules on infringements and penalties for the unlawful acts against conservation of documentary archives or the inappropriate disclosure of information.
34. General Health Law (*Ley General de Salud*)	Articles 74 subsection VIII, 77*bis* 37 subsections X and IX, 100 subsection IV, 103, 103*bis* 3, 114*bis* 1, 161*bis*,166*bis* VI, 166*bis* 15 subsection II, 166*bis* 16, 166*bis* 20, 192*Quintus*, 321*bis*, 316*bis*, 321*bis*–329 and 466	Ministry of Health, the Health Institute for Wellbeing, the Ministry of Public Function and the Federal Judicial Power (*Secretaría de Salud, Instituto de Salud para el Bienestar, Secretaría de la Función Pública y Poder Judicial Federal*)	Right to confidentiality of psychiatric information, confidentiality of beneficiaries of the Health Institute for Wellbeing, confidentiality of the genetic data and donors of organs, tissues and cells. Right to informed consent

Title of the Law	*Provision Number(s)*	*Enforcement Authorities*	*Scope of the Provision(s)*
35. General Law of Education (*Ley General de Educación*)	Articles 30 subsection XV, 159, 170 subsection XXV and 171	Ministry of Education, Ministry of Public Function and Federal Judicial Power (*Secretaría de Educación Pública, Secretaría de la Función Pública y Poder Judicial Federal)*	Incorporates provisions on personal data protection within educational plans and programmes. Obligation of authorities to take measures to protect personal data in verification visits to education centres. It also includes rules on infringements and penalties for unlawful disclosure and transfers of personal data without the consent of data subjects.
36. Law on Migration (*Ley de Migración*)	Articles 78 and 140 subsection I	National Migration Institute, Ministry of Public Function (*Instituto Nacional de Migración, Secretaría de la Función Pública*)	Liability and sanctions of public servants of the National Migration Institute for disclosure of confidential information.
37. Federal Electricity Commission Law (*Ley de la Comisión Federal de Electricidad*)	Articles 27, 29-35, 32 subsection II, 33 subsection VII, 53 subsection III, 96	Federal Electricity Commission (*Comisión Federal de Electricidad*)	Obligation of employees and members of the Executive Board of the Federal Electricity Commission to preserve the confidentiality of the information. Obligations of the internal audit unit to preserve the integrity, confidentiality and availability of the information.

Title of the Law	*Provision Number(s)*	*Enforcement Authorities*	*Scope of the Provision(s)*
38. Law of the Institute for Security and Social Services for State Workers (*Ley del Instituto de Seguridad y Servicios Sociales de los Trabajadores del Estado*)	Articles 7, 10, 13 and 14	Institute for Security and Social Services for State Workers. Ministry of Public Function, Federal Judicial Power (*Instituto de Seguridad y Servicios Sociales de los Trabajadores del Estado, Secretaría de la Función Pública y el Poder Judicial Federal*)	Provisions on the processing of personal data of employees or right holders. Confidentiality of the electronic records. Criminal liability for disclosure of information.
39. Social Security Law (*Ley del Seguro Social*)	Articles 22, 111 A, 251 subsection XXXI	Mexican Social Security Institute and Ministry of Health (*Instituto Mexicano de Seguridad Social y Secretaría de Salud*)	Confidentiality of the information of employers and employees. Safeguards for the protection of electronic medical records.
40. General Law on Forced Disappearance of Persons, Disappearance Committed by Individuals and the National Missing Persons Search System (Ley General en materia de desaparición forzada de personas, desaparición cometida por particulares y del Sistema Nacional de Búsqueda de Personas)	Articles 63, 102-110, 111-118, 119-129	National Prosecutor's Office, National Search Commission, National Center for Crime Prevention and Citizen Participation, and other public security institutions (Fiscalía General de la República, Comisión Nacional de Búsqueda, Centro Nacional de Prevención del Delito y Participación Ciudadana y demás instituciones de seguridad pública)	Provisions on the processing of personal data contained in the National Registry of Disappeared or Missing Persons, the National Registry of Unidentified Deceased Persons and the National Forensic Data Bank
41. Federal Law of the Rights of Contributor (*Ley Federal de los Derechos del Contribuyente*)	Articles 10 and 24	Ministry of Finance (SHCP) and Public Credit, Tax Administration Service (Secretarçia de Hacienda y Crédito Público y Servicio de Administración Tributaria)	Obligation for tax authorities to keep the confidentiality of the information of the taxpayers

Title of the Law	*Provision Number(s)*	*Enforcement Authorities*	*Scope of the Provision(s)*
42. Law on Savings and Popular Credit (*Ley de Ahorro y Crédito Popular*)	Articles 34, 36*bis* 2, 36*bis* 3 subsection I, 122*bis*, 124 and 136	SHCP and Public Credit, Bank of Mexico, National Commission for the Protection and Defense of Financial Service Users (Secretaría de Hacienda y Crédito Público, Banco de México, Comisión Nacional para la Protection y Defensa de los Usuarios)	Obligations and exception for financial corporations of the popular sector to keep the confidentiality of financial activities and operations in order to protect the privacy of clients
43. Law for the Promotion of Citizen Confidence (Ley de Fomento a la Confianza Ciudadana)	Articles 4–9	SE, National Commission for Regulatory Improvement	Rules on the processing of personal data contained in the Registry of Promotion of Citizen Confidence
44. Law on Refugees, Complementary Protection and Political Asylum (Ley sobre Refugiados, Protección Complementaria y Asilo Político)	Articles 5 subsection VI, Articles 10, 21, 23, 40 subsection III, 60	Ministry of Interior and Foreign Affairs Ministry (Secretaría de Gobierno y Secretaría de Relaciones Exteriores)	Confidentiality of applicants, refugees, and asylees

Part II. National Data Protection Law

Chapter 1. Background: General Description of the National Data Protection Law (+ Short Presentation of Other Relevant National Legislation)

83. Mexico's regime on data protection is quite broad and complex and is essentially divided into two main areas: (i) private sector data protection; and (ii) public sector data protection.

84. The FLPPDPP and its Regulation govern the collection and processing of personal information by private legal entities at the federal level since 6 July 2010. The FLPPDPP and its Regulation regulate private sector entities located in any of the thirty-two states of the Mexican Republic. The FLPPDPP and its Regulation came into force in different phases as shown in Table 3.

Table 3 Implementation Phases of the FLPPDPP and Its Regulation

Statute	*Date of Entry into Force*	*Obliged Parties*	*Activities*
FLPPDPP	6 July 2010	INAI, SE	INAI and SE had the obligation to draft the regulation of the law.
Regulation of the FLPPDPP	6 July 2011	The Executive power through INAI and SE, data processors and data controllers and data subjects	The Regulation came into force. Data controllers must have privacy notices in place and should have appointed a Privacy Officer responsible for the protection of personal data under the law.

Statute	*Date of Entry into Force*	*Obliged Parties*	*Activities*
FLPPDPP	6 January 2012	INAI, SE, companies, data processors, data controllers and data subjects	Data subjects may exercise Access, Rectification, Correction, Omission (ARCO) rights under Chapter IV and initiate the rights protection procedure under Chapter VII of the FLPPDPP. Data processors and data controllers must have all the necessary technical and legal mechanisms in place in order for data subjects to exercise such rights.

85. As previously mentioned in paragraph 58, the GLPPDPGPSI regulates the collection, use and processing of personal information exclusively in possession of government and public sector entities in Mexico. The *GLPPDPGPSI* has been in force since 27 January 2017. This law governs public entities at the federal, state and municipal level, as well as any authority, entity, agency or organization of the Executive, Legislative and Judicial branches, autonomous bodies, political parties, trusts and public funds.

This *monograph will specifically cover the provisions contained in the FLPPDPP and its Regulation* and its enforcement by the national data protection authority INAI. A general summary of the main provisions of the *GLPPDPGPSI* will be covered in Part X, Chapter 6 of this monograph.

Chapter 2. Scope of the National Law (Material, Personal, Territorial)

86. Unlike the GDPR, the FLPPDPP does not specifically establish the material and territorial scope of the law. Article 1 only mentions that the law is of general application nationwide. However, the Regulation of the FLPPDPP does establish the subject matter of the FLPPDPP, as well as its territorial scope, as follows.

§1. Subject Matter

87. Pursuant to Article 3, the purpose or subject matter of the Regulation of the FLPPDPP is to apply to the processing of personal data found on physical or electronic media that make possible access to personal data according to specific criteria, regardless of the form or method of its creation, type of media, processing, storage, or organization.

The Regulation does not apply when disproportionate periods of time or activities are required in order to obtain access to personal data.

Pursuant to Article 3(V) of the FLPDPPP, personal data may be in numerical, alphabetical, graphic, photographic, acoustic or any other form concerning an identified or identifiable individual.

§2. Territorial Scope

88. Pursuant to Article 4, the Regulation of the FLPPDPP will be obligatory for all processing when:

(i) it is carried out in an establishment of the data controller located in Mexico;
(ii) it is carried out by a data processor, regardless of its location, on behalf of a data controller established in Mexico;
(iii) the data controller is not established in Mexico but is subject to Mexican laws as a consequence of entering into a contract or under international law; and
(iv) the data controller is not established in Mexico and uses means located in Mexico, unless such means are used only for transit purposes that do not involve processing. For purposes of this subsection, the data controller shall provide the necessary means to comply with the obligations imposed by the Law, its Regulation, and other applicable rules and regulations with respect to the processing of personal data. For this purpose, the data controller shall appoint a representative or implement the mechanism that it considers appropriate, provided that by means of this, it is ensured that the data controller will be able to effectively comply with the obligations that are imposed by law on individuals and corporate bodies processing personal data in Mexico.

89. When the data controller is not located in Mexico, but the data processor is, the latter shall be subject to the provisions related to the security measures contained in Chapter III of the Regulation of the FLPPDPP. In the case of individuals, the establishment shall mean the location of their main place of business or one that is used to conduct their activities or their home.

90. In the case of corporate entities, the establishment shall mean the location of the principal management of the business; in the case of corporate entities residing abroad, the location of the principal management of the business in Mexico, or in the absence thereof, the one appointed by them or any fix premise that allows actual or real performance of an activity.

§3. Exemptions to Scope of Applicability

91. Article 5 sets forth that the Regulation shall not be applicable to the following information:

(i) with respect to corporate entities;
(ii) with respect to individuals as businessmen and women and professionals; and
(iii) with respect to individuals who provide services for a corporate entity or individual engaged in business and/or providing services consisting only of their first names and surnames, the position or post they hold, as well as some of the following data concerning employment: physical address, electronic address, telephone and fax numbers; provided that this information is used only for purposes of representing the employer or contractor.

Chapter 3. Concepts and Definitions

92. The FLPDPPP and its Regulation contain a list of definitions that are used to provide for a better understanding and interpretation of both instruments.

93. Article 3 of the FLPDPPP enlists a total of nineteen definitions, while Article 2 of the Regulation enlists thirteen additional definitions. The definitions contained in the Regulation are the following:

(i) *Departments*: Those established in Article 26 of the Federal Public Administration Organizational Law.
(ii) *ARCO rights*: The rights of access, rectification, cancellation and objection.
(iii) *Digital environment*: The environment made up of the combination of hardware, software, networks, applications, services, or any other technology of the information society that allows for the exchange or computerized or digitalized processing of data.
(iv) *Exclusion list*: Database intended to record free of charge the refusal of the data subject to have his personal data processed.
(v) *Administrative security measures*: Combination of actions and mechanisms to establish the management, support, and review of the security of information at an organizational level, the identification and classification of information, as well as the creation of awareness by personnel and their education and training in the area of protection of personal information.
(vi) *Physical security measures*: Combination of actions and mechanisms, whether or not using technology, intended to:
  (a) prevent unauthorized access or damage to or interference with physical installations, critical areas of the organization, equipment and information;
  (b) protect mobile, portable, or easily removable equipment located inside or outside premises;
  (c) provide maintenance to equipment containing or storing personal data so as to ensure their availability, proper working order, and integrity; and
  (d) guarantee the erasure of data in a secure manner;
(vii) *Technical security measures*: Combination of activities, controls, and mechanisms with measurable results that use technology to ensure that:
  (a) access to logical databases or to information in logical format is by identified and authorized users;
  (b) the access referred to in the previous paragraph is only so that the user may carry out the activities required by his position;
  (c) actions to acquire, operate, develop, and maintain secure systems;
  (d) management of communications and computerized resources used for the processing of personal data.
(viii) *Identifiable individual*: Any individual whose identity can be determined, directly or indirectly, by any information. An individual will not be deemed identifiable when in order to obtain his identification, disproportionate periods of time or activities are required.

(ix) *Transmission*: Communicating personal data between a data controller and a data processor, within or outside of Mexico.

(x) *Electronic medium*: Storage medium that can be accessed only by means of the use of a device with electronic circuits that process its contents in order to examine, modify or store personal data, including microfilms.

(xi) *Physical medium:* Storage medium intelligible by sight, in other words, which does not require any device to process its content in order to examine, modify or store personal data; and

(xii) *Suppression*: Activity consisting in eliminating, erasing, or destroying personal data, once the blocking period has elapsed, under security measures previously established by a data controller.

Part III. General Principles

94. Like most data protection laws, the FLPPDPP and its Regulation contain data protection principles which were mainly adopted from the privacy principles of *OECD Privacy and Data Protection Guidelines* and the *APEC Privacy Framework*. It is important to note that the FLPPDPP and its Regulation were enacted before the revision of the OECD Privacy and Data Protection Guidelines of 2013. Although the OECD did not make any specific reforms or amendments to the national principles, said organization did provide further guidelines and recommendations in particular with respect to the principle of 'Accountability' and how this principle should be extended and interpreted in the current technological context, a situation that INAI has not yet followed or implemented within the scope of interpretation of the FLPPDPP and its Regulation.

Chapter 1. Data Protection Principles

95. The FLPPDPP and its Regulation contain a chapter on general principles that data controllers must observe and adhere to when processing personal information These principles are: (i) lawfulness, (ii) consent, (iii) notice, (iv) quality, (v) purpose, (vi) loyalty, (vii) proportionality and (viii) accountability.

§1. Lawfulness

96. Article 7 of the FLPPDPP states that personal data must be collected and processed in a lawful manner in accordance with the provisions established by the law and other applicable regulations. Personal data must not be obtained through deceptive or fraudulent means. The FLPPDPP sets forth a common law figure relating to the reasonable expectation of privacy understood as the trust any one person places in another for personal data provided to be processed pursuant to any agreement of the parties in the terms established by this law.

97. Article 10 of the Regulation stipulates that the principle of lawfulness requires the data controller to ensure that processing follows and complies with the provisions of Mexican and international law.

§2. Consent

98. The FLPPDPP expressly regulates how consent should be obtained, which is one of the essential requirements for the processing of personal data. Article 8 of the FLPPDPP stipulates that all processing of personal data will be subject to the consent of the data subject, except as otherwise provided in the law. Said article establishes that consent will be considered expressed when it is communicated verbally, in writing, by electronic or optical means or via any other technology, or by unmistakable indications.

It shall be understood that the data subject tacitly consents to the processing of his data, once the privacy notice has been made available to him, and as long as he does not express objection.

In addition, Article 8 stipulates that financial or asses data will require the express consent of the data subject, except as provided in Articles 10 and 37 related to various hypotheses such as when the data is available in publicly available sources, in emergency situations, for health care and provision of medical services and domestic and international transfers, among others. Consent may be revoked at any time without retroactive effects being attributed thereto. For the revocation of consent, the data controller must establish the mechanisms and procedures for such action in the privacy notice.

Article 9 of the FLPPDPP establishes that in the case of sensitive personal data (race, ethnic origin, health status, genetic information, religious beliefs, union affiliation, sexual preference), the data controller must obtain express written consent from the data subject for its processing, through either the handwritten signature of the data subject, an electronic signature, or any authentication mechanism established for such a purpose.

Databases containing sensitive personal data may not be created without justification of their creation for purposes that are legitimate, concrete and consistent with the explicit objectives or activities pursued by the regulated party.

Article 10 of the FLPPDPP establishes the following exceptions for obtaining consent for processing of personal data: (i) when any law so provides; (ii) when the data is contained in publicly available sources; (iii) when the personal data is subject to a prior dissociation procedure; (iv) when it has the purpose of fulfilling obligations under a legal relationship between the data subject and the data controller; (v) in emergency situations that could potentially harm an individual in either his person or property; (vi) when it is essential for medical attention, prevention, diagnosis, health care delivery, medical treatment or health services management; (vii) when the data subject is unable to give consent in the terms established by the General Health Law and other applicable laws, and the processing of data is conducted by a person subject to a duty of professional secrecy or an equivalent obligation, or (vii) through a judgment issued by a competent authority.

99. The Regulation of the FLPPDPP regulated consent in a broader form. Article 11 stipulates that the data controller must obtain consent for the processing of personal data unless it is not required under Article 10 of the FLPPDPP. The request for consent shall refer to a specific purpose or purposes, provided in the privacy notice.

Further, when personal data are obtained personally or directly from the data subject, consent shall be obtained prior to the processing.

I. Main Features of Consent

100. Article 12 of the Regulation provides the forms to obtain tacit or express consent. Pursuant to that article, consent shall be:

(i) free: without error, bad faith, violence or fraud that may affect the expression of the will of the data subject;
(ii) specific: refers to one or several specific purposes that justify its processing; and
(iii) informed: the data subject must previously know from the privacy notice the processing purpose of his personal data and the consequences of granting his consent.

Express consent must also be unequivocal; in other words, there should be sufficient elements that unquestionably demonstrate that it was granted.

II. Tacit Consent

101. Article 13 of the Regulation stipulates that unless the FLPPDPP requires the express consent of the data subject, tacit consent will be valid, as a general rule, pursuant to Articles 11 and 12 of the Regulation.

III. Request for Tacit Consent

102. Article 14 of the Regulation provides that when the data controller seeks to collect personal data directly or personally from the data subject, it shall previously make available to the data subject a privacy notice which shall contain a mechanism by which, as the case may be, the data subject may state his refusal to allow the processing of his personal data for purposes different from those that are necessary and that create a legal relationship between the data controller and the data subject.

In those cases in which personal data is obtained indirectly from the data subject and cause a change in the purposes that were consented to in the transfer, the data controller shall make available to the data subject a privacy notice prior to using the personal data. When the privacy notice is not brought to the attention of the data subject directly or personally, the data subject shall have a period of five days to indicate, as the case may be, his refusal to allow the processing of his personal data for purposes which are different from those that are necessary and that create a legal relationship between the data controller and the data subject. If the data subject does not state his refusal to the processing of his data in accordance with the foregoing, it shall be understood that he has given his consent to the processing of his data, unless it is proved otherwise.

When the data controller uses mechanisms through remote or local electronic, optical or other technological means of communication that allow personal data to be obtained automatically and simultaneously at the time the data subject has contact with said mechanisms, at the same time, the data subject must be informed on the use of such technologies, and that personal data will be obtained through these mechanisms, including the form to disable them.

IV. Express Consent Request

103. Article 15 of the Regulation stipulates that the data controller shall obtain the express consent of the data subject when:

(i) it is required by law or regulation;
(ii) concerning financial or property data;
(iii) concerning sensitive data;
(iv) it is requested by the data controller for evidence purpose;
(v) it is so agreed by the data subject and the data controller.

104. Article 16 of the Regulation provides that when express consent is required by law, the data controller shall provide the data subject with a simple and free-of-charge means of giving it, if he so wishes.

V. Exceptions to the Principle of Consent

105. Article 17 of the Regulation stipulates that as provided in Articles 10 section IV and 37 section VII of the FLPPDPP, tacit or express consent will not be required for the processing of personal data when this arises from a legal relationship between the data subject and the data controller.

The previous paragraph shall not apply when the processing of personal data is for purposes different from those that are necessary and create the legal relationship between the data controller and the data subject. In this case, to obtain tacit consent, the data controller shall comply with Article 8, third paragraph of the FLPPDPP and Articles 11, 12, and 13 of the Regulation. With respect to sensitive, financial, or property data, the data controller shall obtain express consent, or as required by the FLPPDPP, express and written consent.

VI. Verbal Consent

106. Article 18 of the Regulation establishes that it is considered that express consent was given verbally when the data subject provides it orally to the data controller in the latter's presence by the use of any technology that permits oral interaction.

VII. Written Consent

107. Article 19 of the Regulation mentions that express consent should be considered as given in writing when the data subject provides it in a document bearing his handwritten signature, fingerprint, or any other mechanism authorized by law. The use of an electronic signature or any other mechanism or procedure established for this purpose and that allows the identification of the data subject and the obtaining of his consent may be considered as expressed consent.

VIII. Proof of Obtaining Consent

108. Article 20 of the Regulation provides that in order to prove that consent has been obtained, the burden of proof will always rest upon the data controller.

IX. Withdrawal of Consent

109. Article 21 of the Regulation provides that the data subject may revoke his consent for the processing of his personal data at any time, and the data controller shall establish simple and free-of-charge mechanisms to permit the data subject to revoke his consent using at least the same medium that he used to provide it, and as long as that the law does not prohibit it.

The mechanisms or procedures established by the data controller to deal with consent revocation requests may not exceed the period provided in Article 32 of the FLPPDPP.

When the data subject requests confirmation that the processing of his personal data has concluded, the data controller shall expressly respond to such request.

If the personal data has been transmitted prior to the date of the revocation of consent and continue to be processed by the data processor, the data controller shall bring the revocation to the attention of the data processor so that he takes the necessary steps to deal with it.

X. Procedure in the Case of a Refusal for Processing

110. Article 22 of the Regulation provides that in case of refusal by the data controller to stop the processing of personal data in the event of a withdrawal of consent, the data subject may present a complaint to INAI in accordance with Chapter IX of the Regulation.

§3. Quality

111. The principle of quality is contained in Articles 11 of the FLPPDPP and 36 of its Regulation. Article 11 of the FLPPDPP establishes that the data controller shall procure that personal data contained in databases are relevant, correct and up-to-date for the purposes for which it has been collected. When the personal data is no longer necessary for the fulfilment of the objectives set forth in the privacy notice and applicable law, it must be cancelled. The controller of the database will be required to remove information relating to non-performance of contractual obligations, after a period of seventy-two months counted from the calendar day on which said non-performance arose.

Article 36 of the Regulation stipulates that the personal data processed by the data controller will meet the principle of quality when they are exact, complete, relevant, correct and up-to-date as required to comply with the purpose for which they are processed.

Personal data are presumed to be complaint with the quality principle when they are directly provided by the data subject until he declares and proves otherwise, or the data controller has objective evidence contradicting the latter.

When the personal data were not obtained directly from the data subject, the data controller must take reasonable measures to comply with the principle of quality in accordance with the type of personal data and the processing conditions.

The data controller must adopt the mechanisms that it considers necessary to ensure that personal data dealt with are exact, complete, relevant, correct and up-to-date so that the truth of the data is not modified, and the data subject may not be affected by this situation.

§4. PURPOSE

112. The purpose principle is contained in Articles 12 of the FLPPDPP and 40 of its Regulation. Article 12 of the FLPPDPP stipulates that the processing of personal data should be limited to fulfilment of the purposes set out in the privacy notice. If the data controller intends to process data for another purpose which may not be compatible or analogous to the purposes set out in the privacy notice, the consent of the data subject shall need to be obtained again.

Article 40 of the Regulation establishes that personal data may be processed only to comply with the purpose or purposes set out in the privacy notice, as provided in Article 12 of the FLPPDPP.

For purposes of the previous paragraph, the purpose or purposes set out in the privacy notice shall be determined, something which will be achieved when with clarity, and without giving rise to confusion and in an objective manner, the purpose for which personal data will be processed is specified.

I. Purpose Differentiation

113. Article 41 of the Regulation provides that the data controller shall identify and distinguish in the privacy notice between the purposes that give rise to and are necessary for the legal relationship between the data controller and the data subject from those that are not.

II. Objection to Processing for Different Purposes

114. Pursuant to Article 42 of the Regulation, the data subject may refuse or revoke his consent, as well as object to the processing of his personal data for purposes different from those that are necessary or that gave rise to the legal relationship between the data controller and the data subject, without this having as a consequence, the termination of the processing for the latter two purposes.

III. Processing for Different Purposes

115. Article 43 of the Regulation stipulates that the data controller may not carry out processing for different purposes that are not compatible or analogous to those for which the personal data was originally collected and which were mentioned in the privacy notice unless:

(i) a law or regulation explicitly allows it;
(ii) the data controller has obtained consent for the new processing.

§5. Proportionality

116. The principle of proportionality is contained in Articles 13 of the FLPPDPP and 45 of its Regulation. Article 13 of the FLPPDPP establishes that processing of personal data shall be necessary, proportionate and relevant to the purposes set out in the privacy notice. Concerning sensitive personal data, the data controller shall conduct reasonable efforts to limit the term of processing so as to obtain the minimum necessary. Article 45 of the Regulation establishes that only personal data that are necessary, appropriate and relevant in connection with the purposes for which they were obtained may be processed.

§6. Minimization

117. The principle of minimization is contained in Articles 13 of the FLPPDPP and 46 of its Regulation. Article 46 of the Regulation stipulates that the data controller shall conduct reasonable efforts to limit the processing of personal data to the minimum necessary in accordance with the purpose of the processing that will take place.

§7. Loyalty

118. The principle of loyalty is contained in Article 15 of the FLPPDPP and Article 44 of its Regulation. Article 15 of the FLPPDPP provides that the data controller has the obligation to inform data subjects concerning the information collected about them and the purposes through the privacy notice. Article 44 of the Regulation mentions that the principle of loyalty establishes the obligation to process personal data giving priority to the protection of the interests of the data subject and the reasonable expectation of privacy, as provided in Article 7 of the FLPPDPP.

Misleading or fraudulent means may not be used to collect and process personal data. There is a fraudulent or deceptive act when:

(i) there is fraud, bad faith or negligence in the information provided to the data subject about the processing;
(ii) the reasonable expectation of privacy of the data subject referred to in Article 7 has been violated; or
(iii) the purposes are not those contained in the privacy notice.

§8. ACCOUNTABILITY

119. The principle of accountability is contained in Articles 14 and 47 of the Regulation. Article 14 of the FLPPDPP stipulates that the data controller shall ensure compliance with the personal data protection principles contained in the FLPPDPP, and shall adopt all necessary measures for their application. The foregoing will apply even when a third party at the request of the data controller has processed this data. The data controller must take all necessary and sufficient measures to ensure that the privacy notice given to the data subject is respected at all times by the data subject or by any third parties with whom it has any legal relationship.

Article 47 of the Regulation establishes that pursuant to Articles 6 and 14 of the FLPPDPP, the data controller has the obligation to protect and be responsible for the processing of personal data found under its custody or in its possession or for those it has communicated to a data processor, whether or not the latter is located in Mexico.

To comply with this obligation, the data controller may use standards, best international practices, corporate policies, self-regulation schemes, or any other mechanism that it determines adequate for such purpose.

§9. MEASURES FOR THE PRINCIPLE OF ACCOUNTABILITY

120. Article 48 of the Regulation establishes that pursuant to Article 14 of the FLPPDPP, the data controller must adopt measures to guarantee the proper processing of personal data, giving priority to the interests of the data subject and the reasonable expectation of privacy.

The measures that may be adopted by the data controller include at least the following:

(i) Prepare privacy policies and programmes that are binding and enforceable within the organization of the data controller.
(ii) Implement a programme of training, updating, and raising the awareness of personnel about obligations in matters of protection of personal data.
(iii) Establish an internal supervision and monitoring system, as well as external inspections or audits to verify compliance with privacy policies.
(iv) Dedicate resources for the implementation of privacy programmes and policies.
(v) Implement a procedure to deal with the risk to the protection of personal data by the implementation of new products, services, technologies and business models, as well as to mitigate them.
(vi) Periodically review the security policies and programmes to determine modifications required.
(vii) Establish procedures to receive and respond to the questions and complaints of data subjects.
(viii) Have mechanisms to comply with privacy policies and programmes, as well as sanctions for a breach thereof.

(ix) Establish measures to protect personal data, in other words, a group of technical and administrative actions that will allow the data controller to ensure compliance with the principles and obligations established by the FLPPDPP and these Regulations.
(x) Establish measures to trace personal data, in other words, actions, measures, and technical procedures that will allow the tracing of personal data while being processed.

§10. Privacy Notice

121. The information principle is addressed in Article 15 of the FLPPDPP which provides that the data controller has the obligation to inform data subjects concerning the information collected about them and the purposes through the privacy notice, as well as Article 23 of the Regulation. The requirements for privacy notices under the FLPPDPP and its Regulation are quite broad and descriptive. The provisions that regulate privacy notices are Articles 16, 17 and 18 of the FLPPDPP and Articles 23–31 of the Regulation. Further, the Regulation of the FLPPDPP provides the use of compensatory measures when it is not possible to communicate the privacy notice to the data subject or when this task requires disproportionate efforts as a result of the number of data subjects.

§11. Privacy Notice Requirements

122. Article 16 of the FLPPDPP establishes that the privacy notice must contain at least the following information:

(i) the identity and domicile of the data controller collecting the data;
(ii) the purposes of the data processing;
(iii) the options and means offered by the data controller to the data subjects to limit the use or disclosure of data;
(iv) the means for exercising the rights of access, rectification, cancellation or opposition, in accordance with the provisions of the FLPPDPP;
(v) the data transfers to be conducted where applicable; and
(vi) the procedure and means by which the data controller will notify data subjects on the changes to the privacy notice, in accordance with the provisions of the FLPPDPP.

Concerning sensitive personal data, pursuant to the last paragraph of Article 16, the privacy notice must expressly provide that it deals with this type of data.

123. Article 24 of the Regulation establishes that the privacy notice must be simple, with the necessary information, expressed in a clear and understandable language, and with a structure and design that facilitates its understanding.

§12. Acknowledgement of the Privacy Notice

124. Article 17 of the FLPPDPP sets out that the privacy notice must be made available to data subjects through print, digital, visual or audio formats or any other technology, as follows:

(i) where personal data has been obtained personally from the data subject, the privacy notice must be provided at the time the data is collected, clearly and unequivocally, through the format by which collection is carried out, unless the notice has been earlier provided;
(ii) where personal data are obtained directly from the data subject by any electronic, optical, audio or visual means, or through any other technology, the data controller must immediately provide the data subject with at least the information referred to in sections I and II of Article 16 of the FLPPDPP, as well as provide the data subject with mechanisms to obtain the full text of the privacy notice.

125. Article 18 of the FLPPDPP provides that where data has not been obtained directly from the data subject, the data controller must notify him of the changes in the privacy notice.

The text of the preceding paragraph is not applicable where processing is done for historical, statistical or scientific purposes.

When it may not be possible to provide the privacy notice to the data subject or where disproportionate efforts are involved in view of the number of data subjects or the age of the data, the data controller may implement compensatory measures with the authorization of INAI pursuant to the Regulation of the FLPPDPP.

§13. Means of Communication of the Privacy Notices

126. Article 25 of the Regulation establishes that in order to communicate privacy notices, the data controller may use physical or electronic formats, verbal means or any other technology, as long as the data controllers comply with the obligation to inform the data subject.

§14. Elements of the Privacy Notice

127. Article 26 of the Regulation establishes that a privacy notice shall contain the items referred to in Articles 8, 15, 16, 33 and 36 of the FLPPDPP, as well as those established in the guidelines referred to in Article 43 subsection III of the FLPPDPP.

§15. Privacy Notice When Personal Data Is Directly Collected

128. Article 27 of the Regulation establishes that when personal data is obtained directly from the data subject, the data controller must immediately provide at least the following information as provided in Article 17 subsection II of the FLPPDPP:

(i) The identity and address of the data controller.
(ii) The purposes of the processing.
(iii) The mechanisms offered by the data controller in order for the data subject to know the privacy notice in accordance with Article 26 of the Regulation.

The last paragraph of Article 27 establishes that immediate communication of the information above mentioned does not exempt the data controller from the obligation to provide mechanisms for the data subject to know the content of the privacy notice, pursuant to Article 26 of the Regulation.

§16. Privacy Notice in Formats with Limited Space

129. Article 28 of the Regulation establishes that the data controller may disclose a privacy notice to the data subject, as provided in Article 27, when collecting personal data by printed means, provided that the space used to obtain personal data is limited and minimum so that the personal data collected are as well minimum.

§17. Privacy Notice When Personal Data Is Indirectly Collected

130. Article 29 provides that when personal data is obtained indirectly from the data subject, the data controller must observe the following conditions in order to communicate the privacy notice to the data subject:

(i) When the personal data are processed for the purpose provided in a consented transfer or have been obtained from a public access source, the privacy notice shall be communicated through the first contact with the data subject; or
(ii) When the data controller wishes to use the data for a purpose different from the one consented, in other words, when a change of purpose is to take place, the privacy notice shall be communicated prior to the use of the data.

§18. Privacy Notice Evidence

131. Article 31 of the Regulation stipulates that in order to show that a privacy notice has been given and communicated in accordance with the principle of information, the burden of proof shall always rest upon the data controller.

§19. Compensatory Measures

132. The FLPPDPP and its Regulation sets out a sui generis measure to fulfil the obligation of communicating the privacy notice to data subjects when this requires a disproportionate effort for data controllers. The use of compensatory measures is contained in Article 18 of the FLPPDPP and Articles 32–35 of the Regulation.

133. Article 32 of the Regulation provides that in accordance with the third paragraph of Article 18 of the FLPPDPP, when it may not be possible to communicate the privacy notice to the data subject or this requires disproportionate efforts given the number of data subjects or the age of the data, the data controller may implement compensatory measures using mass communication media in accordance with the guidelines issued by INAI duly published in the DOF on 18 April 2012.[66] Such guidelines allow the possibility of using the measures established in Article 35 of the Regulation.

According to the second paragraph of Article 32 of the Regulation, cases that do not fulfil the requirements set out in the guidelines issued by INAI will require the express authorization of this authority, prior to the implementation of the compensatory measure, in accordance with the procedure established in Articles 33 and 34 of the Regulation.

§20. Request for Authorization of Compensatory Measures

134. Article 33 of the Regulation mandates that the procedure to obtain authorization from INAI for the use of compensatory measures using mass communication media referred to in the second paragraph of Article 32 shall initiate always at the request of the data controller.

The data controller shall submit his request directly to INAI or by any other means that the institute has authorized for this purpose. The request shall contain the following information:

(i) The name of the data controller requesting the application, and when applicable, the name of his representative, as well as a copy of the official identification proving legal status and the original for comparison. In the case of a representative, a copy of the document proving his right to represent the data controller, as well as the original for comparison.
(ii) Address to receive notifications and the name of persons authorized to receive them.
(iii) The processing to which it is intended to apply the compensatory measure and its principal features, such as purpose; type of personal data processing; if transfers are to take place, details of the data subjects, like age, geographic location, educational and socio-economic level, among others.

66. The General Guidelines for the implementation of Compensatory Measures without express authorization of INAI published in DOF on 18 Apr. 2012 are available at: https://bit.ly/38A5Hid.

(iv) Grounds or justification stating the impossibility of communicating the privacy notice to data subjects or the disproportionate efforts that this would require. The data controller shall state the number of data subjects involved, age of the data, whether or not there is direct contact with the data subjects, and their economic situation.
(v) Type of compensatory measure sought to be used and the length of the period to be published.
(vi) Proposed text for the compensatory measure.
(vii) Documents that the data controller considers necessary to submit to INAI.

§21. Procedure for Authorization of Compensatory Measures

135. As established in Article 34 of the Regulation, INAI shall have a period of ten days following receipt of the request for compensatory measures to issue its decision on the matter. If the INAI does not issue a decision within the period established, the compensatory measure request shall be considered as authorized.

Once the request has been submitted by the data controller to INAI, the latter shall weigh the disproportionate efforts to communicate the privacy notice, taking the following aspects into consideration:

(i) The number of data subjects.
(ii) The age of the data.
(iii) The economic situation of the data controller.
(iv) The geographic area and sector in which the data controller operates.
(v) The compensatory measure to be adopted.

If INAI assesses that the compensatory measure proposed does not comply with the principle of information, it may propose to the data controller the adoption of another compensatory measure different from the one requested by the data controller in its initial request.

The proposal of INAI shall be brought to the attention of the data controller so that it may take a respective and appropriate action within a period not longer than five days from the day following the reception of the notification.

If the data controller does not respond within the mentioned period, INAI shall resolve with the elements contained in the file.

When INAI resolves that the data controller did not justify the impossibility of communicating the privacy notice to the data subject or that this requires disproportionate efforts, the use of compensatory measures shall not be authorized.

Any authorization granted by INAI shall remain valid as long as the circumstances of the authorization of the compensatory measure do not change.

§22. Compensatory Measures Main Features

136. Article 35 of the Regulation provides that mass communication compensatory measures will include the information provided in Article 27 of the Regulation and shall be communicated through privacy notices published in any of the following:

(i) Newspapers of national circulation.
(ii) Local newspapers or specialized journals when it is proven that the data subjects reside in a particular state entity or are part of a particular activity.
(iii) In the website of the data controller.
(iv) Through hyperlinks located in the website of INAI, set up for this purpose, when the data controller does not have its own website.
(v) Informational posters.
(vi) Information spots on the radio.
(vii) Other alternative mass communication media.

Chapter 2. Legal Grounds for Processing Personal Data

137. The legal grounds for processing personal data are established in Articles 6, 7 and 10 of the FLPPDPP and Articles 10 and 11 of the Regulation.

Article 6 of the FLPPDPP establishes that data controllers responsible for the processing of information shall comply with the principles of legality, consent, information, quality, purpose, loyalty, proportionality and accountability.

Article 7 of the FLPPDPP establishes that personal data shall be collected and processed in a lawful manner in accordance with the provisions established in the FLPPDPP and other applicable regulations. The collection of personal data shall not be conducted through deceptive or fraudulent means.

The last paragraph of Article 7 establishes the assumption of the reasonable expectation of privacy of individuals in the processing of personal data. Said assumption entails the trust any individual places in another concerning the processing of his personal which shall be conducted pursuant to any agreement between the parties in the terms established by the FLPPDPP.

Article 10 of the FLPPDPP establishes the criteria in seven sections when consent is not required for the processing of personal data. These criteria are the following:

(i) when any law establishes it;
(ii) when the data is contained in publicly available sources;
(iii) when the personal data is subject to a prior dissociation procedure;
(iv) when it has the purpose of fulfilling obligations under a legal contract between the data subject and the data controller;
(v) when there is an emergency situation that could potentially harm an individual in his person or property;
(vi) when the information is relevant for medical attention, prevention, diagnosis, health care delivery, medical treatment or health services management, where the data subject is unable to give consent pursuant to the General Health Law and other applicable laws, and said processing of data is conducted by a person subject to a duty of professional secrecy or an equivalent obligation; or
(vii) through a judgment issued by a competent authority.

138. Article 10 of the Regulation stipulates that the principle of lawfulness compels the data controller to ensure that processing of information follows and complies with Mexican and international law.

Article 11 mandates that the data controller shall obtain consent for the processing of personal data unless it is not required pursuant to Article 10 of the FLPPDPP. The request for consent shall refer to a specific purpose or purposes provided in the privacy notice.

Chapter 3. Special Categories of Personal Data

139. The regulation of special categories of data or sensitive data is contained in Article 9 of the FLPPDPP and Article 56 of the Regulation.

Article 9 of the FLPPDPP stipulates that concerning sensitive personal data (race, ethnic origin, health status, genetic information, religious beliefs, union affiliation, sexual preference), the data controller shall obtain express written consent from the data subject for its processing. Said written consent may be obtained through the data subject signature, electronic signature, or any authentication mechanism established for such a purpose.

The second paragraph of Article 9 of the FLPPDPP prohibits the creation of databases containing sensitive personal data, unless there is a real justification for legitimate and concrete purposes and consistent with the explicit objectives or activities pursued by the regulated party.

Article 56 of the Regulation establishes that pursuant to the second paragraph of Article 9 of the FLPPDPP, databases containing sensitive personal data may be created only when:

(i) established by a legal mandate;
(ii) it has been justified pursuant to Article 4 of the FLPPDPP;
(iii) the data controller requires it for legitimate and concrete purposes and in accordance with its explicit activities or purposes.

Chapter 4. Terms for Data Preservation

140. The preservation periods of personal data are set forth in Articles 37, 38 and 39 of the Regulation of the FLPPDPP.

Article 37 of the Regulation establishes that the preservation periods for personal data may not exceed those that are necessary to achieve the purposes that justify its processing. The preservation periods shall comply with the law applicable to the subject matter involved and take into account the administrative, accounting, tax, legal and historical aspects of the information. Once the purpose or purposes of processing have been achieved, the data controller shall proceed to cancel the data in its possession by blocking them and subsequent erasure.

§1. Procedure for Preserving, Blocking and Erasure of Personal Data

141. Pursuant to Article 38 of the Regulation, data controllers shall establish and document procedures for the preservation of data, and when applicable for the blocking and erasure of personal data, including periods of preservation thereof, in accordance with Article 37 of the Regulation.

§2. Evidence of Compliance with Preservation Periods

142. Article 39 of the Regulation provides that the data controller shall prove the preservation of personal data, or when applicable, the blocking, erasure, or cancellation in accordance with the periods set forth in Article 37 of the Regulation or through a request of the right to cancellation.

Part IV. Data Subject Rights

143. The FLPPDPP contains a full chapter on the rights of data subjects (Articles 22–27) followed by another chapter on the exercise of the rights of access, rectification cancellation and objection (ARCO rights) (Articles 28–35). The data subject rights regulated under the FLPPDPP and its Regulation are exactly those contained in the *OECD Privacy Guidelines*. However, since the FLPPDPP is a law that was adopted before the GDPR, the law does not specifically regulate the right to profiling and the right to portability. Likewise, the Regulation of the FLPPDPP contains a full chapter on the rights of data subjects further regulating the exercise of said rights (Articles 87–112).

144. Article 22 of the FLPPDPP establishes that any data subject, or, where applicable, his legal representative, may exercise the rights of access, rectification, cancellation and objection provided in the FLPPDPP. The exercise of any of said rights is neither a preliminary requirement nor does it impede the exercise of another right. Personal data shall be safeguarded in such a way so as to allow the exercise of these rights without delay.

It should be noted that, in accordance with the INAI's annual activity reports of 2019 and 2020, men exercise ARCO rights more than women. During the period from October 2018 to September 2019, there were 210 requests of men in contrast with 116 of women. The same pattern is observed in the period from October 2019 to September 2020, in which there were 142 requests from men compared to 82 from women.[67]

67. Cfr. INAI, Prepared Activity Reports to be submitted to the Senate of the Mexican Union Congress. Available at: https://micrositios.inai.org.mx/informesinai/.

Chapter 1. Right to Be Informed

145. Article 112 of the Regulation of the FLPPDPP regulates the processing of decisions made without human intervention. This article provides that when the processing of personal data is part of a decision-making process where there is no human intervention, the data controller must inform the data subject about this situation.

Likewise, the data subject may exercise his right of access in order to know the personal data used as part of the decision-making process, and as the case may be, his right to rectification, when he considers that part of his personal data used is incorrect or incomplete so that, in accordance with the mechanisms implemented by the data controller for this purpose, he can request a reconsideration of the decision made.

Chapter 2. Right of Access

146. Article 23 of the FLPPDPP establishes that data subjects will have the right to access their personal data held by data controller as well as to know the privacy notice to which the processing of data is subject to.

Article 101 of the Regulation establishes that pursuant to Article 23 of the FLPPDPP, the data subject has the right to access his personal data from the data controller, as well as information regarding the conditions and general features of the processing.

Article 102 of the Regulation provides that the obligation to provide access will be considered as complied with when the data controller makes available to the data subject personal data on-site, respecting the period set out in Article 99 of the Regulation, or by issuing photocopies or using magnetic, optical, sound, visual or holographic media, as well as other information technologies contemplated in the privacy notice. The access must be granted in formats which are readable and comprehensive to the data subject.

When the data controller considers it convenient, it may agree with the data subject reproduction media for the information different to those contained in the privacy notice.

Chapter 3. Rights of Rectification

147. Articles 24 of the FLPPDPP and 103 of the Regulation provide that the data subject will have the right to rectify data when inaccurate or incomplete.

Article 104 of the Regulation sets out the requirements to exercise the right to rectification. Said article establishes that the request for rectification must indicate the personal data it refers to, as well as the rectification or correction to be made, and must be accompanied by the documentation proving the admissibility of the request. The data controller may offer mechanisms for the benefit of the data subject to facilitate the exercise of this right.

Chapter 4. Right to Erasure

148. Unlike the GDPR, the right to erasure as such is not specifically provided under the FLPPDPP and its Regulation. Instead, the FLPPDPP and its Regulation provide the right to cancel personal data.

Article 25 of the FLPPDPP establishes that the data subject will have the right to cancel his personal data at any time.

The cancellation of personal data will lead to a blocking period which will be followed by the erasure of the data. The data controller may preserve data exclusively for purposes pertaining to responsibilities arising from the processing. The blocking period will be equivalent to the limitation period for actions arising from the legal relationship governing the processing pursuant to the terms contained in the applicable law.

Once the data have been cancelled, the data subject will be notified.

When personal data have been sent prior to the date of rectification or cancellation and continues to be processed by third parties, the data controller must notify them of the request for rectification or cancellation, so that such third parties may also execute it.

Article 105 of the Regulation provides that cancellation implies stopping the processing of personal information by the data controller, starting from their blockage of data and its subsequent deletion.

Article 106 of the Regulation provides the data subject may request the data controller to cancel his personal data at any time, when he considers that the data is not being processed in accordance with the principles and obligations set out in the FLPPDPP and its Regulation.

The cancellation may be admitted with respect to the whole personal data of the data subject contained in a database, or only part thereof, as originally requested.

149. Article 26 of the FLPPDPP establishes that the data controller will not be compelled to cancel personal data when:

(i) it relates to the parties in a private, social or administrative contract and when they are necessary for its performance and compliance;
(ii) the law requires that they shall be processed;
(iii) hindering judicial or administrative proceedings relating to tax obligations, investigation and prosecution of crimes, or updating of administrative sanctions;
(iv) it is necessary to protect the legal interests of the data subject;
(v) it is necessary to carry out an action on the basis of the public interest;
(vi) it is necessary to fulfil an obligation legally undertaken by the data subject; and
(vii) it is subject to processing for medical diagnosis or prevention or the management of health services, provided such processing is conducted by a health professional subject to a duty of secrecy.

150. Further, Articles 107 and 108 of the Regulation establish the criteria and procedure for the blocking of personal data. Article 108 provides that pursuant to

Article 3 section III of the FLPPDPP, the blocking of data has the purpose of preventing the processing, with the exception of storage, or the possible access by any person, unless otherwise established by law. The blocking period will be until the end of the limitation period or contractual period.

151. Article 107 of the Regulation provides that if the cancellation is granted, and without prejudice of Article 32 of the FLPPDPP, the data controller shall:

(i) establish a blockage period only for the purpose of determining possible responsibilities with respect to the processing, up to the legal or contractual limitation period, and shall notify the data subject or his representative in the reply to the request for cancellation within the period of twenty days set out in Article 32 of the FLPPDPP;
(ii) adopt appropriate security measures for the blockage;
(iii) conduct the blockage within the period of fifteen days set out in Article 32 of the FLPPDPP;
(iv) conduct the respective erasure using the security measures previously established by the data controller once the blocking period has expired.

Chapter 5. Cases on the Right to Erasure (Right to Be Forgotten)

152. The judgment of the Court of Justice of the European Union (CJEU) in the case *Google Spain v. AEPD, Mario Costeja Gonzalez* of 13 May 2014 had an indirect effect in one of the findings of INAI with respect to the exercise of the ARCO rights of data subjects and more in particular with respect to the so-called right to erasure provided in Article 17 of the EU General Data Protection Regulation (GDPR).

153. In February 2007, the magazine *Fortuna* published an article involving allegedly fraud activities of a national transport company Grupo Estrella Blanca and Carlos Sanchez de la Peña. The information contained on said article was indexed in the Google search engine. In July 2014, Mr Sanchez de la Peña requested Google Mexico to delete all the hyperlinks and information where his name appeared linking him with allegedly fraud activities contained in the article published by *Fortuna* Magazine from its search engine.

As a result of a lack of a response from Google, Mr Sanchez de la Peña launched and requested a protection of rights procedure before INAI in September 2014 on the grounds that his rights of cancellation and opposition under the FLDPPPP were not respected.

On 27 January 2015, INAI resolved that Google did not allow the exercise of the right of cancellation and opposition to the processing of personal data of Sanchez de la Peña. INAI stated in its finding that: (i) Google Mexico S. de R.L. is a corporation legally established in Mexico, and it is therefore responsible for the processing of personal data under the FLDPPPP; (ii) Google processes personal data when the information of any individual is placed in its search engine and is indexed on the Internet; (iii) Google shall allow the data subject exercise his rights of opposition and cancellation of personal data effectively under the FLDPPPP.[68]

Subsequently, Google challenged INAI's finding before the Federal Tribunal of Tax and Administrative Justice in February 2015, while *Fortuna* Magazine requested an amparo trial before the Fifteenth Court on Administrative Matters in Mexico City on the grounds that its rights of freedom of expression and to a legal hearing were infringed during the proceedings conducted by INAI. The Federal Tribunal of Tax and Administrative Justice initially rejected the amparo request, and *Fortuna* Magazine challenged the judgment and requested for its revision, which was subsequently assigned to the Seventh Collegiate Circuit Tribunal of the First Assistant Region under file number 355/2016.

On August 2016, said tribunal granted the amparo request to *Fortuna* Magazine (which was legally represented by the Non-Government Organization (NGO) Red en Defensa de los Derechos Digitales (R3D)) on the grounds that its right to due process and legal audience were infringed. R3D argued that the request to remove

---

68. INAI Finding under the File Number PPD.0094/14 Google Mexico S. de R.L. de C.V. is available at: http://inicio.ifai.org.mx/pdf/resoluciones/2014/PPD%2094.pdf (last visited October 2021).

a hyperlink from the article of the magazine constituted a censorship measure and a form of Internet intermediary responsibility that conflicted with the right to freedom of expression.[69]

Based on the latter judgment, INAI's finding should remain without legal effect, and as a result, it could invalidate Google's challenge before the Federal Tribunal of Tax and Administrative Justice and might possibly force INAI to commence a new procedure and resolve accordingly. However, as of the date of publication of the current edition of this monograph, there is no additional information on the status of this case.

69. Red en Defensa de los Derechos Digitales (R3D), '!Ganamos! Tribunal anula resolución del INAI sobre el falso derecho al olvido', 24 Aug. 2016, available at: https://r3d.mx/2016/08/24/amparo-inai-derecho-olvido/ (last visited September 2021).

Chapter 6. Right to Restriction

154. Under Mexican law, the right to restriction is not expressly provided. The FLPPDPP and its Regulation regulate the right to object to the processing of personal data [*see* Chapter 7].

Chapter 7. Profiling

155. Unlike the GDPR, the right to profiling is not expressly regulated in the FLPPDPP and its Regulation. As previously mentioned in Chapter 1, Article 112 of the Regulation of the FLPPDPP regulates the processing of decisions made without human intervention. This article provides that when the processing of personal data is part of a decision-making process where there is no human intervention, the data controller must inform the data subject about this situation. There is only the obligation to inform the data subject when the processing is made through an automatized process where no humans are involved.

Chapter 8. Right to Object

156. Article 27 of the FLPPDPP establishes that data subject will have the right to object to the processing of their personal data at any time and for any legitimate reason. Where this is possible, the data controller may not process the data of the data subject.

157. Article 109 of the Regulation provides that the data subject may object to the processing of his personal data or require the data controller to stop its processing when:

(i) there is a legitimate reason for doing so and when a specific situation so requires it. There should be a justification of fact that, even though the processing is lawful, it must stop in order to continue causing a prejudice to the data subject;
(ii) the data subject needs to state his objection to the processing of his personal data in order to avoid processing for specific purposes.

The exercise of the right to objection may not be applicable in those cases where the processing is necessary to comply with a legal obligation imposed upon the data controller.

158. Article 110 of the Regulation provides that in order to exercise the right to objection, data controllers may prepare their own exclusion lists, which may include the data of the data subjects who have expressed their objection for the procession of their personal data, either for products or those of third parties.

Furthermore, data controllers may prepare common exclusion lists by industry or in general.

In both cases, the registry of the data subject in such lists must be free of charge and shall provide the data subject evidence of registration to the list through mechanisms established by the data controller.[70]

70. INAI created a 'General Guide for Data Subjects' which consists of four main volumes. Volume 3 contains useful information and frequently asked questions concerning the exercise of ARCO rights. *See* INAI, 'Guia para Titulares de Datos Personales. Volumen 3. Los Derechos Arcos', available at: https://home.inai.org.mx/wp-content/documentos/GuiasTitulares/Guia%20Titulares-03_PDF.pdf.

Chapter 9. Data Subject Rights Procedure

159. Chapter VII (Articles 45–58) of the FLPPDPP and Chapter VII (Articles 113–127) of the Regulation set out the rules of procedure of data subject rights before the INAI.

§1. Initiation of the Procedure

160. Article 45 of the FLPPDPP establishes that the procedure will be initiated upon request of the data subject or his legal representative, clearly stating the content of data subject's claim and the provisions of the FLPPDPP that are deemed to be violated. The request must be submitted to INAI within fifteen days from the date of the communication of the data controller's response to the data subject.

161. In the event that the data subject does not receive a response from the data controller, the data protection request may be filed following the deadline for the response to the data controller. In this case, it will be sufficient for the data subject to enclose the document that proves the date on which he filed the request for access, rectification, cancellation or objection.

162. The data protection request will also be valid under the same terms when the data controller does not provide the requested data to the data subject, or when he provides the data in an incomprehensible form, or when refuses to make changes or corrections to the personal data, or when the data subject is not satisfied with the information provided as a result of the incomplete information or when it does not pertain to the information requested.

163. Upon receipt of the data subject rights request by INAI, said institute will forward it to the data controller who shall provide a response within fifteen days, whereby the data controllers may provide any relevant evidence and elaborate formal arguments in writing.

164. INAI shall admit any relevant evidence in the proceeding. INAI may request any other evidence it deems convenient from the data controller. After the conclusion of the evidence proceeding, INAI will notify the data controller so that he can present counterarguments within five days following the notification.

For the due development of the proceedings, INAI shall issue a decision on the data protection request filed, after analysing the evidence and other elements it deems convenient, like those arising from the hearings held between the parties.

The Regulation of the FLPPDPP will provide the form, terms and conditions under which the protection of rights procedure shall be conducted.

§2. FORM

165. Article 46 of the FLPPDPP establishes that the data protection request may be filed in writing or using the electronic system forms provided by INAI for such a purpose. The request shall contain the following information:

(i) the name of the data subject or of his legal representative where applicable, as well as of any interested third party to the request;
(ii) the name of the data controller to whom the request for personal data access, rectification, cancellation or objection was submitted;
(iii) an address to hear and receive notifications;
(iv) the date on which the response from the data controller was acknowledged except where the procedure starts pursuant to Article 50 of the FLPPDPP;
(v) the acts that justify the data protection request; and
(vi) any other relevant aspects that should be brought to the attention of INAI.

166. The form and terms on the accreditation of the identity of the data subject or of the legal representative are set out in the Regulation.

167. The data protection request will include the request and the response that is being challenged or any information that enables its identification where applicable. In case of a lack of response, only the submission request will be necessary.

In case the data protection request has been filed through non-electronic means, it shall include sufficient copies for notification.

§3. TERMS FOR THE RESPONSE

168. Article 47 of the FLPPDPP establishes that the maximum term for the final decision in the rights protection procedure shall be fifty days from the date of the initial request filing. If there is a justified cause, INAI's Plenary may extend the term only once and for an equal length period.

169. Article 48 of the FLPPDPP stipulates that when the protection of rights decision is in favour of the data subject, the data controller will conduct all action required in accordance with the exercise of the rights subject to protection within ten days following the notification or when it may be justified. The data controller shall report on the compliance in writing to INAI within the following ten days.

170. Article 49 of the FLPPDPP establishes that if the data protection request fails to satisfy any of the requirements provided in Article 46 of the FLPPDPP, and where INAI lacks the information to remedy such omissions, the data subject will be instructed, a single time, within twenty working days following the filing of the data protection request, to remedy the omissions within five days. If the instructions are not followed by the deadline, the data protection request will be considered as not filed. The prevention instructions will have the effect of interrupting the term INAI has to issue a decision on the request for data protection.

171. Article 50 of the FLPPDPP provides that INAI will remedy the deficiencies in the complaint request where it may be necessary, as long as it does not modify the original content of the request for personal data access, rectification, cancellation or objection, including the facts or petitions set out therein or in the data protection request.

§4. Effects of the Decision

172. Article 51 of the FLPPDPP provides that INAI's decisions may:

(i) dismiss or reject the data protection request as inadmissible; or
(ii) confirm, reverse or amend the response of the data controller.

173. Article 52 of the FLPPDPP provides that the data protection request will be rejected and not admissible when:

(i) INAI lacks jurisdiction;
(ii) INAI has previously known the data protection request for the same act and issued a final decision with regard to the same petitioner;
(iii) any petition or legal action filed by the data subject is pending before a competent court that may have the effect of amending or revoking the act in question;
(iv) the data protection request is offensive or irrational; or
(v) it has been filed out of the term.

174. Article 53 of the FLPPDPP provides that the request for data protection will be discarded when:

(i) the data subject dies;
(ii) the data subject expressly withdraws from the request;
(iii) grounds for inadmissibility arise followed after admission of the data protection request;
(iv) for any cause concerning the end of the effect of the subject matter.

175. Article 54 of the FLPPDPP allows INAI at any time in the procedure to seek conciliation between the data subject and the data controller.

If a conciliation agreement is reached between the two parties, this will be in writing and will have a binding legal effect. The data protection request will become moot, and INAI will verify the compliance of the respective reached agreement.

The conciliation procedure shall be governed by the Regulation of the FLPPDPP.

176. Article 55 of the FLPPDPP provides that in case of a lack of response from the data controller to a data protection request concerning the exercise of the rights of access, rectification, cancellation or objection, INAI will serve notice to the data controller to demonstrate that it has responded in a timely manner to the request within a term of ten days. If the response satisfies the request, the data protection request will be considered without merit and INAI must discard it.

In the second case scenario, INAI will issue its final decision based on the content of the original request, and the response of the data controller referred to in the preceding paragraph.

If the decision of INAI referred to in the preceding paragraph determines that the request is admissible, the data controller will follow immediate compliance without charge to the data subject. The data controller shall bear all costs resulting from the respective reproduction.

177. Article 56 of the FLPPDPP provides that an individual could file a petition for annulment of the decisions issued by INAI with the Federal Tax and Administrative Court.[71]

178. Article 57 of the FLPPDPP provides that all the judgment decisions of INAI may be released in public versions. INAI will delete any references to the data subject, which may identify or make him identifiable.

179. Article 58 of the FLPPDPP provides that data subjects who feel they have suffered a harm or damage to their property or rights as a result of a breach of the provisions of the FLPPDPP by the data controller or data processor may exercise the rights they deem convenient for purposes of any applicable compensation, in the terms of the relevant law.

180. As previously mentioned, Chapter VII (Articles 113–127) of the Regulation specifies in further detail the form, terms, conditions, requirements and the legal procedure to exercise data subject rights before INAI.

---

71. The Second Chamber of the Supreme Court of Justice issued a judgment (jurisprudential thesis) on 9 Oct. 2020, resolving that the federal administrative trial (Juicio Contencioso Administrativo Federal) is legally inadmissible against the decisions issued by INAI in the area of data protection in possession of private entities pursuant to Art. 56 of the FLPPDPP. According to the reasoning of the Second Chamber of the Supreme Court of Justice of the Nation, the nullity judgment is inadmissible, because the constitutional reform on data protection for private entities published in DOF on 7 Feb. 2014 provides a better instance for the challenge of these resolutions for a private individual through the amparo trial (juicio de amparo). *See* Semanario Judicial de la Federacion, Decima Epoca, Segunda Sala, 9 de Octubre de 2020, available in Spanish at: https://bit.ly/3xVo1gH.

Part V. Duties of Controllers and Processors

Chapter 1. National Rules Regarding Duties of Controllers

181. The FLPPDPP and its Regulation set out the specific duties and obligations of data controllers for the collection and processing of personal information from data subject.

Article 14 of the FLPPDPP establishes a general compliance rule for data controllers to ensure the observance and compliance with data protection principles and to adopt necessary measures for their application. Said compliance rule applies even when a third party at the request of the data controller processes personal data. The data controller shall take all necessary and sufficient action to provide data subjects with a privacy notice, and any third parties to whom the data subject has any legal relation shall respect the terms and conditions established in the privacy notice.

Chapter 2. National Rules Regarding Joint Controllers

182. The FLPPDPP and its Regulation do not contain special rules or criteria for joint controllers. However, the Regulation of the FLPPDPP establishes legal obligations for the collection and processing of information of services, applications and infrastructure providers based in the cloud.

§1. Processing of Personal Data of Cloud Computing Services

183. Article 52 of the Regulation establishes that for the processing of personal data in services, applications and infrastructure based in the cloud where the data controller adheres to the same general contractual conditions or clauses, the data controller may only use those services when the cloud provider complies at least with the following:

(a) Provide policies in place to protect personal data equivalent to the applicable principles and duties set out in the FLPPDPP and its Regulation.
(b) Provide transparent policies for subcontracting including information about the service that is being provided.
(c) Avoid including conditions for the provision of the service that authorize or permits to assume the ownership of the information concerning the service provided.
(d) Keep the confidentiality of the personal data concerning the service provided.

Data controllers shall incorporate at least the following mechanisms for:

(a) disclosing changes in its privacy policies or on conditions of the service provided.
(b) allowing the data controller to limit the type of processing of personal data of the service provided.
(c) establishing and maintaining adequate security measures for the protection of personal data of the service provided.
(d) ensuring the erasure of personal data once the service to the data controller finishes and allowing the data controller to retrieve information.
(e) preventing access to personal data to those who do not have access credentials or in the event of a request made from a competent authority. The data controller needs to be duly informed.

The data controller may not be able to use services which do not ensure the respective protection of personal data.

The last paragraph of Article 52 of the Regulation establishes a definition of cloud computing, which is defined as '*the model for the external provision of computer services upon demand that involves the supply of infrastructure, platform or software distributed in a flexible manner, using virtual procedures, on resources dynamically shared*'.

Government agencies in cooperation with INAI shall issue guidelines for the processing of personal data based on 'cloud computing'.

Chapter 3. National Rules with Regard to Processors

184. Article 49 of the Regulation establishes a definition of data processor. A data processor is an individual or corporate body, public or private, which is not part of the data controller, that alone or together with others processes personal data on behalf of the data controller as a result of a legal relationship linking him and delimiting the scope of its action for the provision of a service.

§1. Obligations of the Data Processor

185. Pursuant to Article 50 of the Regulation, the data processor has the following obligations with respect to the processing conducted on behalf of the data controller:

(i) Process personal data only according to the data controller's instructions.
(ii) Avoid processing personal data for a different purpose other than the one instructed from the data controller.
(iii) Implement the security measures pursuant to the FLPPDPP, the Regulation, and other applicable laws and regulations.
(iv) Keep the confidentiality regarding the processing of personal data.
(v) Delete personal data subject to processing after the legal relationship with the data controller has concluded or upon instructions of the data controller, as long as there is no legal requirement that mandates for the preservation of personal data.
(vi) Avoid the transfer of personal data unless the data controller so determines, the communication arises from a subcontracting, or if so required by a competent authority.

The agreements between the data controller and data processor related to the processing of personal data shall be consistent with the respective privacy notice.

186. Article 51 of the Regulation stipulates that the relationship between a data controller and data processor shall be formalized through contractual clauses or other legal instrument elected by the data controller that enables it to accredit its existence, reach and content.

187. The Regulation of the FLPPDPP sets out obligations to processors regarding national and international data transfers, and for the outsourcing and subcontracting of services between data controllers and data processors.

§2. Transfers of Personal Data

188. Article 53 of the Regulation establishes that national and international transfers of personal data between a data controller and a data processor do not need to be informed to the data subject in order to obtain his consent.

The data processor will be considered as a data controller, concerning all the obligations of the data controller when it:

(i) uses the personal data for a different purpose other than the one authorized by the data controller.
(ii) conducts a transfer without following the instructions of the data controller.

The data processor shall not be responsible when upon express instructions from the data controller transmits the personal data to another data processor appointed by the latter, to which it had entrusted the provision of a service, or transfers the personal data to another data controller pursuant to the Regulation.

§3. Subcontracting of Services

189. Article 54 of the Regulation stipulates that any subcontracting of services by the data processor which involves the processing of personal data shall be authorized by the data controller and shall be made in his name and on behalf of the controller.

Once the authorization has been obtained, the data processor shall formalize the relationship with the subcontractor through contractual clauses or any other instrument that allows its existence, scope and content.

The subcontracted individual or corporate entity will assume the same obligations that are established for the data processor under the FLPPDPP and its Regulations and other applicable laws.

The data processor has the obligation of proving that the subcontracting was conducted with the authorization of the data controller.

190. Article 55 of the Regulation establishes that when the contractual clauses or legal instruments that formalized the relationship between the data controller and the data processor establish that the data processor may conduct the subcontracting of services, the authorization referred to in Article 54 will be considered as granted according to terms established in such instruments.

In case that the subcontracting was not provided in the contractual clauses or legal instruments, the data processor must obtain the authorization from the data controller prior to subcontracting.

Chapter 4. Security Obligations

191. Security obligations for data controllers and data processors are established in Article 19 of the FLPPDPP and Chapter III (Articles 57–66) of the Regulation.

Article 19 of the FLPPDPP stipulates that data controllers that process personal data shall establish and maintain physical and technical administrative security measures that enable the protection of personal data from damage, loss, modification, destruction or unauthorized use, access or processing.

Data controllers shall not adopt lower security measures than those they use to manage their own information. The risk involved, potential consequences for the data subjects, the sensitivity of the data and the technological development will be taken into account.

192. Article 57 of the Regulation establishes that both the data controller and the data processor shall establish and keep administrative, physical and technical security measures for the protection of personal data pursuant to the FLPPDPP regardless of the processing system used. Security measures are defined as a control or group of security controls to protect personal data. This is without detriment of the laws and regulations in force concerning security issued by the competent authorities for the corresponding sector when they provide a higher protection for data subjects than the one provided in the FLPPDPP and its Regulation.

§1. Security Functions

193. Article 59 of the Regulation stipulates that in order to establish and ensure effective security measures, the data controller may adopt its own security measures or may contract them with an individual or corporate entity.

§2. Factors to Determine Security Measures

194. Article 60 of the Regulation provides that the data controller shall determine the security measures applicable to the processing of personal data, taking into account the following factors:

(i) The inherent risk by category of personal data.
(ii) The sensitivity of the processing of personal data.
(iii) The technological development.
(iv) The possible consequences of a security breach for the data subjects.

In addition, the data controller shall take the following factors into account:

(i) The number of data subjects.
(ii) Previous vulnerabilities found in the processing systems.

(iii) The risk for the potential quantitative or qualitative value that the processing personal data may have to an unauthorized third party seeking possession of the data.
(iv) Other factors that may have an impact upon the level of risk or that result from other applicable laws or regulations to the data controller.

§3. Adoption of Actions for the Security of Personal Data

195. Article 61 of the Regulation establishes that the data controller shall take the following actions in order to establish and maintain the security of personal data:

(i) Prepare an inventory of personal data and processing systems.
(ii) Determine the duties and obligations of individuals who process personal data.
(iii) Have a risk analysis of personal data consisting of identifying dangers and estimating the risks to the personal data.
(iv) Establish the applicable security measures to personal data and identify those effectively implemented.
(v) Conduct security breaches, which consist of the differences between existing security measures for the protection of personal data and those that are missing.
(vi) Draft a work plan for the implementation of the missing security measures deriving from the security breach analysis.
(vii) Conduct reviews and audits.
(viii) Train the staff who process personal data.
(ix) Keep a record of the data protection storage means.

The data controller shall have an inventory of the security measures adopted.

§4. Update of Security Measures

196. Article 62 of the Regulation established that data controllers shall provide updates to the document setting out security measures when the following events occur:

(i) When changes to the security measures or processes are made for its ongoing improvement, arising as a result of the revisions of the security policy of the data controller.
(ii) When substantial modifications are made to the processing arising from a change in the level of risk.
(iii) When processing systems are breached, as provided in Article 20 of the FLPPDPP and Article 63 of the Regulation.
(iv) When a different impact on the personal data occurs.

Regarding sensitive personal data, data controller shall review and if necessary update the security inventory once a year.

§5. Security Breaches

197. Article 20 of the FLPPDPP establishes that any security breaches from the data controller occurring at any stage of the processing that materially affects the property or moral rights of the data subjects shall be immediately reported to the data subject, so that the data subject may take appropriate action to defend his rights.

198. Article 58 of the Regulation establishes that pursuant to Article 65 section III of the FLPPDPP, whenever a breach of the security of personal data occurs, INAI may take into consideration the compliance of its recommendations in order to determine the reduction of the respective fine.

199. Article 63 of the Regulation provides that breaches to the security of personal data in each processing phase may be the following:

(i) Loss or unauthorized destruction.
(ii) Theft, misplacement or unauthorized copying.
(iii) Unauthorized use, access or processing.
(iv) Damage and unauthorized change or modification.

§6. Notification of Security Breaches

200. Article 64 of the Regulation provides that the data controller shall inform the data subject of any breaches that significantly affect his non-pecuniary rights or property. Once the data controller has acknowledged the breach and it has adopted actions to remedy the scale of the breach without undue delay, the affected data subjects may adopt and take respective measures.

§7. Information Disclosure to Data Subjects as a Result of a Security Breach

201. Article 65 of the Regulation establishes that the data controller shall at least inform the data subject on the following:

(i) The nature of the breach.
(ii) The personal data compromised.
(iii) Recommendations to the data subject concerning measures that he can adopt to protect his interests.
(iv) Corrective actions implemented on an immediate basis.
(v) The means where the data subject may obtain further information.

§8. Corrective Measures as a Result of a Security Breach

202. Article 66 of the Regulation provides that in case of a security breach of personal data, the data controller shall make an analysis of the causes that originate it and implement corrective, preventive and improvement measures in order to improve the adequacy of the respective security measures to avoid a repetition of a security breach.

INAI published in June 2018 a guide titled: 'Recommendations for the Management of Security Breaches of Personal Data'.[72] The purpose of this guide is to assist data controllers in complying with the provisions on security of personal data and the obligation of notification to data subjects affected as a result of a data breach contained in the FLPPDPP and its Regulation. The guide contains a description of the recommended procedures to generate a response plan to security breaches to assist data controllers in mitigating the security of personal data based on international standards and general accepted practices.

72. INAI, 'Recommendations for the Management of Security Breaches of Personal Data', June 2018, available at: https://home.inai.org.mx/wp-content/documentos/DocumentosSectorPrivado/Recomendaciones_Manejo_IS_DP.pdf.

Chapter 5. Data Protection Officer or Similar Functions

203. Pursuant to Article 30 of the FLPPDPP, data controllers shall appoint an individual or department responsible for data protection. The appointed individual or department shall process the request of data subjects in order to allow for the exercise of the rights provided in the FLPPDPP and its Regulation. Likewise, data controllers shall promote the protection of personal data within their organizations.

204. Neither the FLPPDPP nor its Regulation establishes specific duties and obligations of the appointed individual or department responsible for data protection. INAI published in August 2016 a document titled: 'Recommendations for the Appointment of the Person or Department Responsible for Data Protection'.[73]

Among INAI's main recommendations regarding the appointed individual responsible for data protection are: (i) experience on protection of personal data; (ii) have a strategic hierarchical position within the organization; (iii) have sufficient funding; (iv) have experience and knowledge in the subject matter; (v) have vision and leadership; and (vi) have good organization and communication skills.

73. INAI, 'Recommendations for the Appointment of the Person or Department responsible for Data Protection', August 2016, available at: https://home.inai.org.mx/wp-content/documentos/DocumentosSectorPrivado/RecomendacionesDesignar.pdf.

Part VI. Codes of Conduct and Certification

§1. Codes of Conduct

205. The use of codes of conduct as an additional mechanism to protect personal data is not specifically regulated under the FLPPDPP and its Regulation.

In the context of electronic commerce, Article 24 section IX*bis* of the FCPL provides that the Profeco has the duty to promote in coordination with the SE, the formulation, diffusion and use of codes of ethics among companies. Said codes of ethics shall include the principles provided by the FCPL concerning electronic commerce transactions with consumers.

The Mexican Internet Association (AI.MX) has promoted a trust seal known as '*Sello de Confianza* Asociación Internet.MX' among its membership since 2007. The main purpose of this trust seal is to enhance security of e-commerce transactions. National institutions and businesses adhering to AI.MX trust seal represent an acknowledgement that:

(i) they have a legal establishment in Mexico;
(ii) their websites are trustworthy and ethically responsible; and
(iii) they comply with privacy and information policies based on the national legal framework on data protection and international privacy guidelines.

206. The AI.MX which forms part of the World Trustmark Alliance currently has two major trust seals. One trust seal on electronic commerce which is used to acknowledge trust and security for online transactions, and another trust seal on personal data that acknowledges that websites of companies have a privacy policy in place and that comply with the terms and conditions and additional elements provided in the FLPPDPP and its Regulation including a mediation service in case of a dispute.[74]

207. The AI.MX has issued more than 175 trust seals on personal data and 54 trust seals on e-commerce to national and multinational companies established in Mexico until August 2021.[75]

74. Further information on the trust seals of AI.MX is available at: https://sellosdeconfianza.org.mx/.
75. Info regarding the total amount of trust seals issued by AI.MX is available at: https://sellosdeconfianza.org.mx/?op=listas.

§2. CERTIFICATIONS

208. The FLPPDPP and its Regulation provide specific rules for binding self-regulation arrangements that allow for the certification of data controllers concerning their practices on data collection and processing.

I. Self-Regulatory Schemes

209. Articles 44 of the FLPPDPP and 79 of the Regulation provide that individuals or legal entities may enter into agreements among them or with national, foreign civil or governmental organizations on self-regulatory schemes that may help to complement compliance with the provisions of the FLPPDPP and its Regulation. The self-regulatory schemes shall include mechanisms to measure the effectiveness of the protection of personal data, consequences and effective corrective measures in case of non-compliance.

Self-regulatory schemes may take the form of codes of ethics or good professional practice, trust seals or other mechanisms. They shall include specific rules or standards enabling the harmonization of data processing conducted by adherents and facilitate the exercise of the rights of data subjects. The notification of such schemes shall be made simultaneously to the relevant sectoral authorities and INAI.

Chapter V of the Regulation (Articles 79–86) sets forth additional rules of self-regulatory schemes.

II. Purpose of Self-Regulatory Schemes

210. Article 80 of the Regulation provides that self-regulation arrangements may take the form of codes of ethics or codes of good professional practice, trustmarks, privacy policies, corporate privacy rules among other mechanisms that include specific rules or standards. Self-regulation arrangements have the following main objectives:

(i) Support the compliance with the accountability principle contained in the FLPPDPP and its Regulation.
(ii) Establish qualitative procedures and practices in the field of protection of personal data to complement the provisions of the FLPPDPP.
(iii) Encourage data controllers to establish policies, procedures and best practices for compliance with the principles of the protection of personal data, safeguarding the privacy and confidentiality of the personal information in their possession.
(iv) Encourage data controllers to keep records or certifications regarding the compliance with the provisions of the FLPPDPP on a voluntary basis, and acknowledge data subjects about their commitment to the protection of personal data.

(v) Identify data controllers with privacy policies aligned with the implementation of the principles and rights of the FLPPDPP, as well as labour competencies for the respective compliance of their obligations in the subject matter.
(vi) Facilitate coordination with different self-regulation schemes recognized internationally.
(vii) Facilitate transfers with data controllers that have self-regulation arrangements such as safe harbour.
(viii) Promote the commitment of data controllers with accountability obligations and the adoption of internal policies consistent with external criteria, as well as the fostering of mechanisms to implement privacy policies, including tools, transparency, continuous internal supervision, risk assessment, external inspections and remedy systems.
(ix) Foster alternative dispute resolution mechanisms among data controllers, data subjects and third parties, such as conciliation and mediation.

The arrangements shall be binding upon the parties who decide to join. However, joining the arrangements shall be voluntary.

III. Incentives for Self-Regulation

211. Article 81 of the Regulation provides that when a data controller adopts and complies with a self-regulation arrangement, INAI shall take into consideration this circumstance when deciding upon the respective reduction of a fine in the event of a failure of compliance with the FLPPDPP or its Regulation. Additionally, INAI may establish other incentives for the adoption of self-regulation arrangements, as well as mechanisms that facilitate administrative proceedings.

IV. Minimum Requirements of Self-Regulation Schemes

212. Article 82 of the Regulation provides that self-regulation schemes shall include the standards issued by SE, in cooperation with INAI for the correct development of this type of self-regulation mechanisms and measures by adopting at least the following:

(i) The type of arrangement agreed. This may take the form of ethics codes, good professional practice codes, trustmarks or any other arrangement that enable data subjects to identify data controllers committed to the protection of personal data.
(ii) The scope of application of self-regulation arrangements.
(iii) The procedures or mechanisms to be used to ensure the effective protection of personal data of the contracting parties, and to measure its effectiveness.
(iv) Internal and external supervision and monitoring systems.
(v) Training programmes for parties processing personal data.
(vi) Mechanisms for the exercise of data subjects rights.

(vii) Identification of adhering individuals or legal entities that enable the identification of data controllers that comply with the requirements of a self-regulation arrangement and their commitment to the protection of personal data.
(viii) Implementation of effective corrective measures in case of non-compliance.

V. Certification on Personal Data Protection

213. Article 83 of the Regulation provides that binding self-regulation arrangements may include the certification on protection of personal data for data controllers.

If a data controller decides to follow a certification procedure, the certification shall be granted by a certifying individual or corporate entity different than the data controller in accordance with the guidelines and the standards set out in Article 43 section V of the FLPPDPP for this purpose.

VI. Accredited Individuals and Legal Entities

214. Article 84 of the Regulation provides that individuals and legal entities accredited as certifiers shall have as a main duty the certification of privacy policies, programmes and procedures voluntarily set by data controllers are followed in practice while ensuring that the processing and the adopted security measures adopted are necessary for the protection. For this purpose, certifiers may adopt mechanisms such as inspections and audits.

The procedure for accreditation of certifiers referred to in the previous paragraph shall be conducted in accordance with the guidelines provided in Article 43 section V of the FLPPDPP. The certifiers shall safeguard their independence and impartiality when granting the certificates, as well as the compliance with the requirements and criteria established in said guidelines.

VII. Self-Regulation Guidelines

215. Article 85 of the Regulation specifies that the self-regulation guidelines referred to in Article 43 section V of the FLPPDPP shall include mechanisms for the accreditation and revocation of the accreditation of certifying individuals and legal entities, as well as their activities; general criteria for granting certificates on the protection of personal data; and the procedure for the notification of binding self-regulation arrangements.

VIII. Registry of Self-Regulation Guidelines

216. Article 86 provides that the self-regulation arrangements notified pursuant to the last paragraph of Article 44 of the FLPPDPP shall be part of a registry administered by INAI that will include the entities and organizations that comply with the requirements established under the guidelines provided in Article 43 section V of the FLPPDPP.

IX. Self-Regulation Standards from the SE

217. The SE published in DOF of 29 May 2014 *Self-Regulation Standards on Protection of Personal Data*, which is an instrument that substituted the Standards for the Correct Development of Binding Self-Regulatory schemes originally published by INAI in DOF of 17 January 2013.[76]

The main purpose of the self-regulation standards of SE is to establish rules, criteria and procedures for the correct development and implementation of binding self-regulatory schemes on the protection of personal data for the private sector referred to in Article 44 of the FLPPDPPP and Articles 79–86 of the Regulation of the FLPPDPPP.

The self-regulatory standards are binding in the whole Mexican Republic, and they are used for the validation and acknowledgement of certifications on data protection for private sector entities duly recognized by INAI.

The binding self-regulatory schemes contain a total of eighty-nine articles divided into five chapters and four transitory provisions. INAI officially commenced to receive validation requests from data controllers and to issue binding self-regulatory mechanisms since April 2015. The Registry of Self-Regulatory Standards (better known as REA) has also been operating since April 2015.

218. Currently, there is only one national accreditation entity endorsed and recognized by INAI, Entidad Mexicana de Acreditación A.C.

219. Likewise, there are two certifying organizations officially endorsed and recognized by INAI responsible for the certification of data controllers and data processors under binding self-regulatory schemes:

Normalización y Certificación Electrónica, S.C (NYCE); and Global Certification Bureau, S.A.

76. The Self-Regulation Standards on Protection of Personal Data published by the Ministry of Economy are available at: http://www.dof.gob.mx/nota_detalle.php?codigo=5346597&fecha=29/05/2014.

220. Telefonica Mexico was the first company that obtained a certification on personal data protection in August 2015 from the certifying organization NYCE with acknowledgement of INAI.[77]

221. As of September 2021, more than fifty-seven companies have received a data protection certification from NYCE with the acknowledgement of INAI.[78]

77. El Financiero, 'Telefónica México obtiene certificado en materia de protección de datos', 13 Aug. 2015, available at: http://www.elfinanciero.com.mx/empresas/telefonica-mexico-obtiene-certificado-en-materia-de-proteccion-de-datos.html.
78. The complete list of companies that have obtained a certification on personal data protection under the current Self-Regulatory Standards is available at: http://rea.inai.org.mx/_catalogs/masterpage/Sec6_1.aspx.

Part VII. International Transfers

Chapter 1. General Principles

222. International data transfers are regulated in Chapter V (Articles 36 and 37) of the FLPPDPP and Chapter IV (Articles 67–76) of the Regulation. Unlike the GDPR, international transfers of data from a third country to Mexico do not require an adequacy decision from the national data protection agency INAI.

223. Article 36 of the FLPPDPP establishes that where the data controller intends to transfer personal data to domestic or foreign third parties other than the data processor, the data controller shall provide them with the privacy notice and the purposes to which the data subject agreed to the processing of his data.

Data processing shall be conducted according to the terms agreed in the privacy notice. The privacy notice shall contain a clause indicating whether the data subject agrees or not to the transfer of his data. Likewise, the third-party receiver shall accept the same obligations pertaining to the data controller that transferred the data.

224. Article 37 provides that domestic or international data transfers may be conducted without the consent of the data subject when the following hypotheses occur:

(i) where the transfer is conducted pursuant to a law or treaty to which Mexico is a party;
(ii) where the transfer is necessary for the prevention or medical diagnosis, health care services, medical treatment or the management of health services;
(iii) where the transfer is conducted to holding companies, subsidiaries or affiliates under common control of the data controller, or to a parent company or any company belonging to the same group of the data controller, operating under the same internal processes and policies;
(iv) where the transfer is necessary by virtue of a contract executed or to be executed in the interest of the data subject, the data controller and a third party;
(v) where the transfer is necessary or legally required to safeguard a public interest or for the administration of justice;
(vi) where the transfer is necessary for the acknowledgement, exercise or defence of a right in a judicial proceeding; and
(vii) where the transfer is necessary to maintain or fulfil a legal relationship between the data controller and the data subject.

§1. Scope of Transfers of Personal Data

225. Article 67 of the Regulation provides for the scope of 'a transfer', which is referred to the communication of personal data to a party other than the data subject, data controller or data processor, within or outside national territory.

§2. Transfer Conditions

226. Article 68 of the Regulation provides that any transfer of personal data whether national or international is subject to the consent of the data subject, with the exceptions provided in Article 37 of the FLPPDPP. The transfer shall be informed to the data subject through the privacy notice and shall be limited to the purpose that justifies it.

§3. Compliance with Transfer Obligations

227. Article 69 of the Regulation provides that for purposes of demonstrating that either a national or international transfer was conducted in accordance with the FLPPDPP and its Regulation, the burden of proof shall at all times rest upon the data controller that made the transfer and upon the receiver of the personal data.

§4. Transfers Within the Data Controller's Same Group

228. Article 70 of the Regulation provides that for purposes of transfers of personal data among holding companies, subsidiaries or affiliates under the common control of the data controller's same group, or to a parent company or to any company belonging to the same group of the data controller, the mechanism to ensure that the receiver of the personal data complies with the provisions of the FLPPDPP and its Regulation, and other applicable laws and regulations, may be the existence of binding internal corporate rules to protect personal data as long as said rules comply with the requirements of the FLPPDPP, the Regulation, and other applicable laws and regulations.

§5. Specific Conditions Applicable to National Transfers

229. Article 71 of the Regulation provides that in order to conduct transfers of personal data within national territory, the data controller shall comply with Article 36 of the FLPPDPP and Article 68 of the Regulation.

§6. Receiver of Personal Data

230. Article 72 of the Regulation provides that the receiver of personal data shall be regulated as a data controller in accordance with the FLPPDPP and its Regulation, and it shall process personal data in accordance with terms contained in the privacy notice communicated by the transferring data controller.

§7. Formalization of National Transfers

231. Article 73 of the Regulation provides that the transfer shall be formalized through a mechanism that acknowledges that the transferring data controller communicated to the receiving data controller the conditions under which the data subject consented to the processing of his personal data.

§8. Specific Conditions Applicable to International Transfers

232. Article 74 of the Regulation provides that international transfers of personal data will be possible when the receiver of the personal data assumes the same obligations pertaining to the data controller that transferred the personal data, regardless of Article 37 of the FLPPDPP.

§9. Formalization of International Transfers

233. Article 75 of the Regulation provides that the data controller that transfers personal data may be able to use contractual clauses and other legal instruments which contain at least the same obligations as those to which the data controller transferring personal data is subject to, as well as the conditions under which the data subject consented to the processing of his personal data.

§10. INAI's Opinion Concerning Transfers

234. Article 76 of the Regulation provides that data controllers, if they deem it necessary, may request INAI's opinion on whether international transfers they conduct comply with the FLPPDPP and its Regulation.

Chapter 2. Transfers in the Context of International Agreements (E.g., Mutual Legal Assistance Treaties)

235. Mexico is a party to a wide number of international treaties and mutual legal assistance treaties in the field of criminal law. Concerning mutual legal assistance treaties on criminal matters, each treaty contains specific rules on how the information on crime perpetrators and victims of crime may be used and exchanged among law enforcement and government agencies. However, there is not yet a specific law or regulation in Mexico that regulates the collection and processing of personal information for law enforcement entities and authorities of the criminal justice system. The GLPPDPGPSI regulates national law enforcement bodies, but its scope and provisions are not as detailed like, for example, the EU Data Protection Law Enforcement Directive (EU) 2016/680[79] and Spain's Organic Law 7/2021 of 26 May on the protection of personal data processed for purposes of prevention, detection, investigation and adjudication of criminal penalties and execution of criminal conduct.[80]

236. As previously mentioned in paragraph 30 of this monograph, Mexico has a trade agreement with the United States and Canada (USMCA) which replaced the former NAFTA of 1994. The USMCA has been in force since 1 July 2020.

237. Article 19.11 of the USMCA establishes prohibitions and restrictions to the cross-border transfer of information, including personal information, by electronic means if this activity is for the conduct of the business of a covered person.

Paragraph 2 of Article 19.11 establishes that nothing in said Article shall prevent a party from adopting or maintaining a measure inconsistent with paragraph 1 necessary to achieve a legitimate public policy objective, provided that the measure:

(a) is not applied in a manner which would constitute a means of arbitrary or unjustifiable discrimination or a disguised restriction on trade; or
(b) does not impose restrictions on transfers of information greater than are necessary to achieve the objective.

79. Directive (EU) 2016/680 of the European Parliament and of the Council of 27 Apr. 2016 on the protection of natural persons with regard to the processing of personal data by competent authorities for the purposes of the prevention, investigation, detection or prosecution of criminal offences or the execution of criminal penalties, and on the free movement of such data, and repealing Council Framework Decision 2008/977/JHA, available at: https://bit.ly/3Ajwmfa.

80. Ley Orgánica 7/2021, de 26 de mayo, de protección de datos personales tratados para fines de prevención, detección, investigación y enjuiciamiento de infracciones penales y de ejecución de sanciones penales was published in BOE number 126 of 27 May 2021, available at: https://www.boe.es/eli/es/lo/2021/05/26/7/con.

Part VIII. Enforcement

Chapter 1. Supervisory Authorities

238. The FLPPDPP and its Regulation set out two national agencies responsible for the enforcement of data protection for private sector entities, the INAI and the SE. INAI is the sole institution responsible for the general compliance of the FLPPDPP and its Regulation and the protection of data subject rights. The SE is responsible for the diffusion of knowledge and expertise on data protection for the commercial sector exclusively.

Chapter 2. Composition

239. The INAI is an independent institution, with legal personality and assets and with an official legal domicile in Mexico City. The Plenary is the highest management body. It is composed of seven Commissioners, elected upon convocation of the Mexican Senate.

The members of INAI's Plenary have a seven-year mandate, without the possibility of re-election. During their term, they are not allowed to take any other job, position or commission, with the exception of unpaid positions in educational, scientific or charitable institutions.

The Chair Commissioner is elected by the members of the Plenary session through a secret vote. The Chair Commissioner has the legal representation of INAI and constitutes the official link between the governing body and the executive structure of INAI with the aim to coordinate the execution and development of institutional policies and programmes.

The activities of INAI's Governing Body are regulated by the Constitution, the Federal Law of State Entities and its Regulations, as well as by the Decree that creates the INAI. The Governing Body meets as often as required by the own administrative functions of INAI. This may not be less than four times a year.

Chapter 3. Competence, Tasks and Powers

§1. INAI

240. Articles 38 and 39 of the FLPPDPP set out the specific powers, tasks and competencies of INAI.

Article 38 of the FLPPDPP provides that the main purpose of INAI is the dissemination of knowledge on the right to personal data protection across the Mexican society, the promotion of the exercise to data protection, and ensure the correct enforcement of the provisions of the FLPPDPP and those deriving there from, in particular, those related to the compliance of obligations of the parties regulated under the FLPPDPP.

241. Article 39 of the FLPPDPP provides that INAI has the following attributions:

(i) Enforce and verify compliance with the provisions of the FLPPDPP, within the scope of its competence and with the exceptions provided therein.
(ii) Interpret the law within the sphere of the administrative system.
(iii) Facilitate technical support to the data controllers who so request it for the compliance of the obligations established by the FLPPDPP.
(iv) Issue opinions and recommendations pursuant to the applicable provisions of the FLPPDPP for purposes of its functioning and operation.
(v) Disseminate standards and international best practices on information security considering the nature of the data, the processing purposes, and the technical and financial capacities of the data controller.
(vi) Hear and issue decisions concerning data protection rights and verification procedures established under the FLPPDPP and issue fines accordingly.
(vii) Cooperate with national and international organizations and supervisory authorities in the field of data protection.
(viii) Submit an annual activity report to National Congress.
(ix) Participate in international fora on data protection.
(x) Conduct studies on impact assessments on privacy prior to the implementation of new modalities of processing of personal data or the material modification of existing types of processing.
(xi) Develop, promote and disseminate reviews, studies and research in the field of protection of personal data held by private parties and provide training to the obligated parties.
(xii) Any other responsibilities under the FLPPDPP and other applicable laws.

§2. Ministry of Economy

242. Articles 40–44 of the FLPPDPP establish the powers and competencies of the SE. The SE is responsible for the diffusion of knowledge and expertise on data protection for the commercial sector among national and international entities of the private sector, as well as for the issuance of guidance of self-regulation standards on data protection.

243. Article 41 of the FLPPDPP provides that SE shall be responsible for the dissemination of information concerning obligations on the protection of personal data among national and international private companies with commercial activity in Mexico. SE shall promote best business practices on protection of personal data as an input for the digital economy, and the national economic development as a whole.

244. Article 42 of the FLPPDPP provides that concerning commercial databases, the regulations issued by SE shall only apply to automated databases or that are part of an automatization process.

245. Article 43 of the FLPPDPP enlists the attributions of SE:

(i) Disseminate knowledge regarding the protection of personal data in the commercial sphere.
(ii) Foster good commercial practices in the field of personal data protection.
(iii) Issue relevant guidelines concerning the content and scope of privacy notices in cooperation with INAI.
(iv) Issue, within the scope of its competence, the general administrative provisions referred to in Article 40 of the FLPPDPP in cooperation with INAI.
(v) Establish adequate guidelines for the correct development of self-regulatory mechanisms and measures referred to in Article 44 of the FLPPDPP, including the promotion of Mexican Standards and Official Mexican Standards in cooperation with INAI.
(vi) Maintain consumer registries in the field of personal data and verify their correct operation.
(vii) Execute agreements with chambers of commerce, associations and business organizations in the field of personal data protection.
(viii) Design and implement policies and coordinate studies for the modernization and the efficient operation of electronic commerce, as well as to promote the development of the digital economy and information technologies in the field of personal data protection.
(ix) Participate in national and international trade-related fora in the field of personal data protection, or in any event of a commercial nature.
(x) Support the execution of events and activities that contribute to the diffusion of personal data protection.

Chapter 4. Remedies

246. Besides the procedure for the protection of data subject rights analysed in Chapter 8 of this monograph, the FLPPDPP and its Regulation contain specific rules for the procedures of investigation and verification that INAI may conduct against data controllers and data processors that infringe any of the provisions of the FLPPDPP and its Regulation.

247. The procedures of Investigation and Verification of the private sector are regulated under Articles 59–60 of the FLPPDPP and Articles 128–139 of the Regulation. INAI's General Directorate of Investigation and Verification is the area responsible for the conduction of these procedures. The main objective of these procedures is to ensure that data controllers process personal data correctly pursuant to the LFPDPPP, its Regulation and other applicable regulations.

248. The Investigation and Verification procedures apply when INAI decides to launch its own-initiative enquiry or when a data subject wants to report an unlawful processing of personal data from a data controller of the private sector. The own-initiative investigations only apply on the event of non-compliance with a prior resolution regarding the procedure of the protection of data subject rights, or when well-founded and motivated reasons exist to presume a violation of Federal Law. The procedures launched on the basis of a petition or complaint imply that the complainant has sufficient knowledge and evidence that the data controller is not complying with the LFPDPPP, its Regulation and other applicable regulations, or that the data controller is not processing personal data respecting the principles and obligations provided for in the national data protection legislation.

Concerning the Investigation and Verification procedures regulated under the LFPDPPP, there is no particular deadline for a data subject to submit a complaint before INAI.

§1. Investigation Procedure

249. The Investigation Procedure will have a maximum duration of ninety business days. This term may be extended once, up to an equal period, as long as there is a cause that justifies it.[81]

Once the complaint has been filed to INAI, it is then submitted to the GDIV, which will analyse it, and in case of finding a deficiency, it will notify the complainant who presented it so that he can provide the additional information that is required with the purpose to be able to conduct the corresponding investigation. When the complaint does not have any deficiencies, INAI shall communicate it to

81. The Investigation Procedure described in this section was obtained from INAI, 'Guia para Titulares de los Datos Personales Volumen 4. Procedimientos de Datos Personales ante el INAI' p. 23, available at: https://home.inai.org.mx/wp-content/documentos/GuiasTitulares/Guia%20Titulares-04_PDF.pdf.

the complainant, in order to request him to provide further information and relevant elements that may legally complete his complaint.

The GDIV may issue requests to the complainant in order to complete his file, and once the file is duly completed, the GDIV will proceed to the analysis and study of the file. The GDIV may issue either of the following statements:

- Determination Statement: Issued by the GDIV if it considers that the data controller did not violate principles or obligations contained in the LFPDPPP and its Regulation.
- Start of the Verification Procedure Statement: Issued when the GDIV assumes that the data controller has incurred actions or omissions that lead to a probable cause of breach of the principles or obligations provided in the LFPDPPP and its Regulation.

250. According to the INAI's annual work reports, the highest number of investigation files opened for non-compliance with the LFPDPPP occurred during the period between October 2017 and September 2018. In total, 1,256 investigations were opened during that period in contrast with the 531 files opened between October 2018 and September 2019 or the 469 files opened between October 2019 and September 2020.[82]

The sectors that have faced the highest number of investigation processes since 2016 to 2020 are professional, scientific and technical services, the financial and insurance sector, information in the mass media, as well as the retail trade sector. Only in the period between October 2016 and September 2017, the health and social assistance sectors were ranked in third place with a total of forty-seven processes initiated.[83]

§2. Verification Procedure

251. The GDIV is also in charge of the Verification Procedure.[84] This procedure has a maximum duration of 180 business days, and it may be extended once, up to an equal period, as long as there is a cause that justifies it.

Once the Statement on the Start of the Verification Procedure has been issued, it shall be communicated to the complainant and the data controller. This procedure may be developed as follows:

82. Cfr. INAI, Activity Prepared Reports submitted each year to the Senate of the Mexican Union Congress. Available at: https://micrositios.inai.org.mx/informesinai/.
83. *Ibid.*
84. The Verification Procedure described in this section was obtained from INAI, 'Guía para Titulares de los Datos Personales Volúmen 4. Procedimientos de Datos Personales ante el INAI', p. 24, available at: https://home.inai.org.mx/wp-content/documentos/GuiasTitulares/Guia%20Titulares-04_PDF.pdf.

- *Through information requests*: The GDIV shall conduct these requests through official communications addressed to the data controller, so that within five business days after the acknowledgement of the data controller, he can submit any relevant evidence concerning the processing of personal data and express his opinion regarding the initial complaint and the Verification Procedure established against him.
- *Through verification visits*: The GDIV shall conduct these visits. This procedure consists of making on-site visits to the establishment of the data controller, so that the GDIV can obtain relevant information about the processing of personal data from the data controller. The on-site visits will have a maximum duration of ten days.

Once the INAI, through the GDIV, considers that there are sufficient elements to determine whether there was indeed a violation of the principles or obligations of the LFPDPPP from the data controller, the Plenary of INAI (through the seven Commissioners) shall issue the respective judgment. The judgment may establish the initiation of the procedure for the imposition of fines, or the conclusion of the Verification Procedure.

In accordance with Article 138 of the Regulation, either the data subjects or the data controller may challenge the final judgment on the Verification Procedure from INAI before the Federal Court of Administrative Justice (FCAJ). However, the Supreme Court of Justice has established case law in the sense of declaring inadmissible the challenge of the INAI's decisions before the FCAJ, in order to preserve its constitutional autonomy.[85] However, this jurisprudence does not exclude the possibility to challenge jurisdictionally the decisions of the INAI.

252. According to the INAI's annual work reports,[86] the highest number of verification procedures was carried out in the period between October 2018 and September 2019, with a total of 774 cases. This number contrasts significantly with the number of procedures carried out in previous years: 75 (2015-2016), 120 (2017-2018) and 63 (2019-2020).[87]

The sectors that have faced the highest number of verification procedures are the professional, scientific and technical services, the financial and insurance sector,

85. National Supreme Court of Justice, Tenth Epoch, Register 2022203, Jurisprudence 2a./J. 31/2020 (10a.), Federal Weekly Judiciary Gazette, Book I, Volume II, October 2020, p. 668. Available at: https://sjf2.scjn.gob.mx/detalle/tesis/2022917. Available at: https://sjf2.scjn.gob.mx/detalle/tesis/2022203.
86. Cfr. INAI, Activity Prepared Reports submitted each year to the Senate of the Mexican Union Congress. Available at: https://micrositios.inai.org.mx/informesinai/.
87. The number of verification procedures during the period between October 2016 and September 2017 is not available in the respective Activity Report elaborated by the INAI. The period between October 2019 and 2020 is not considered representative, given the special circumstances due to the COVID-19 pandemic and the suspension of deadlines in the procedures.

information in the mass media, the retail trade sector, and the health and social assistance sector. All of which are consistent with the sectors previously investigated by the authority, referred to in paragraph 226.[88]

However, it should be noted that the greatest number of investigations and verifications carried out by the INAI is found in the sector of professional, scientific and technical services, which presents a significant difference among the other sectors. More than 55% of the investigations and more than 76% of the verifications are concentrated in this sector.

88. Cfr. INAI, Activity Prepared Reports submitted each year to the Senate of the Mexican Union Congress. Available at: https://micrositios.inai.org.mx/informesinai/.

Chapter 5. Liabilities and Security Vulnerabilities

253. The LFPDPPP and its Regulation do not specifically address aspects concerning contractual liability aspects for the processing of personal information.

254. Chapter XI (Articles 67–69) of the LFPDPPP regulates crimes concerning security vulnerabilities and unauthorized processing of personal data.

255. Article 67 of the LFPDPPP establishes an imprisonment term from three months to three years for any person – being authorized to process personal data for profit purposes – who causes a security vulnerability affecting the databases under his custody.

256. Article 68 provides an imprisonment term from six months to five years to any person who processes personal data deceitfully with the aim to obtain an unlawful profit, while taking advantage of a mistake of the data subject or the person authorized to transmit such data.

257. Article 69 provides that concerning sensitive personal data, the penalties may be increased up to double.

258. It is important to point out that INAI does not have the power to levy penalties as a result of these offences. However, INAI has the obligation to file criminal reports to the competent law enforcement authorities.

259. Chapter III (Articles 63–66) of the Regulation sets forth obligations for data controllers to secure personal data, including the obligations to notify security vulnerabilities and corrective measures (*see* paragraphs 134–137 of this monograph).

Chapter 6. Infractions and Penalties

260. Chapter X (Articles 63–69) of the LFPDPPP establishes fines for failing to comply with the obligations contained in the law, and Chapter X (Articles 140–144) of the Regulation sets out the rules of procedure for the imposition of fines against data controllers deriving from the data subject rights protection or verification procedures.

261. Among the conducts of the data controller that may constitute infractions under the LFPDPPP are the following:

- Not complying with the data subject's request for access, rectification, cancellation or opposition to the processing of his personal data, without a well-founded reason.
- Acting negligently in providing a response and follow-up to ARCO rights requests.
- Declaring unlawfully the non-existence of personal data, when such data totally or partially exist in the database of the data controller.
- Processing personal data in contravention of the principles established in the LFPDPPP.
- Not including any or all mandatory informative elements in the privacy notice.
- Maintaining inaccurate personal data when it is attributable to the data controller, or not conducting the respective rectifications or cancellations.
- Not complying with the duty of confidentiality.
- Changing substantially the original purpose of the data processing.
- Transferring data to third parties without communicating to them the privacy notice that contains the limitations to which the data subject conditioned the disclosure of his data.
- Breaching the security of databases, premises, computer programs or equipment, when it is attributable to the data controller.
- Conducting the transfer or assignment of personal data, outside of the scope permitted by the law.
- Collecting or transferring personal data without the express consent of the data subject, in cases where this is required.
- Collecting data in a deceptive and fraudulent way.
- Continuing with the illegitimate use of personal data when the conclusion has been requested from INAI or the data subjects.
- Obstructing the acts of verification of the supervisory authority.
- Processing personal data in a way that affects or prevents the exercise of ARCO rights.[89]

262. In accordance with the annual activity reports elaborated by the INAI, the most recurrent infractions to the LFPDPPP are the contravention of the principles

89. INAI, 'Guía para Titulares de los Datos Personales Volúmen 4. Procedimientos de Datos Personales ante el INAI', pp. 29 and 30, available at: https://home.inai.org.mx/wp-content/documentos/GuiasTitulares/Guia%20Titulares-04_PDF.pdf.

established in the law, the collection or transfer of personal data without the consent of the data subject, the lack of privacy notices, and the obstruction of verification acts of the authority. In addition, the most frequently violated principles are those of lawfulness, accountability, notice and consent.[90]

§1. Procedure for the Imposition of Fines

263. For the imposition of the respective fines arising from the aforementioned infractions, INAI conducts a Procedure for the Imposition of Fines.[91] This type of procedure is an administrative procedure where only the alleged offender who violated any of the principles or provisions of the LFPDPPP and its Regulation participates. Therefore, the party who submitted a complaint or a request for the protection of data subject rights is no longer involved in this procedure. The purpose of Procedure for the Imposition of Fines is to determine the fine that the Plenary of INAI will impose on the data controller.

The Plenary of INAI determines the initiation of the Procedure for the Imposition of Fines in the resolutions deriving from either the Rights Protection Procedure or the Verification Procedure.

The General Directorate for the Protection of Rights and Sanctions is the administrative unit of INAI in charge of conducting the Procedure for the Imposition of Fines.

The five different stages of the Protection of Rights and Sanctions procedure are the following.

I. Start

264. The procedure begins with the issuance of a Statement agreement that is notified to the data controller that infringes the law. Said statement agreement contains a description of the facts of the presumed infringement. Then, the data controller is requested to present evidence, and respond to each of the facts within the term of fifteen business days.

II. Evidence

265. Once the term granted to the alleged offender to provide a response to the initial Statement Agreement and to offer legal evidence has elapsed, INAI issues another Statement acknowledging the evidence admitted, and ordering the validation of the evidence admitted.

90. Cfr. INAI, Activity Prepared Reports submitted each year to the Senate of the Mexican Union Congress. Available at: https://micrositios.inai.org.mx/informesinai/.

91. The Procedure for Imposition of Fines described in this section was obtained from INAI, 'Guía para Titulares de los Datos Personales Volúmen 4. Procedimientos de Datos Personales ante el INAI' pp. 30–31, available at: https://home.inai.org.mx/wp-content/documentos/GuiasTitulares/Guia%20Titulares-04_PDF.pdf.

In the event that the alleged data controller does not make use of that right, INAI shall issue another statement that acknowledges that the data controller's right to present further evidence is not legally possible.

III. Allegations

266. Once the stage for the presentation of evidence has concluded, INAI grants a period of five business days to the data controller so that the data controller, if deemed necessary, may present his allegations in writing.

IV. Closing of Instruction

267. Once the term for submitting allegations has concluded, INAI issues another statement in order to finalize the instruction procedure so that INAI's Plenary issues the final resolution of the procedure. The Procedure for the Imposition of Fines has a duration of fifty business days. This term may be extended only once, up to an equal period, when there is a cause that justifies it.

V. Resolution

268. If there is consensus on the final resolution among INAI's Plenary, then the Commissioners endorse it, and it is finally notified to the data controller.

§2. Fines and Penalties

269. The penalties for the aforementioned infractions imposed by INAI may be the following:[92]

- The warning request from INAI so that the data controller may execute the acts requested from the data subject, in the terms provided by the LFPDPPP, when the infringement is the result of not complying with the request of the data subject for the exercise of ARCO rights, without good reason.
- Fine from 100 to 160,000 days of minimum wage (currently the daily value of the Measure and Actualization Unit (UMA)) in force in Mexico City, in the cases provided in sections II–VII of Article 63 of the LFPDPPP.
- Fine from 200 to 320,000 days of minimum wage in force in Mexico City (currently the daily value of the UMA) in the cases provided in sections VIII–XVIII of Article 63 of the LFPDPPP.

---

92. The Fines and Penalties described in this section were obtained from INAI, 'Guía para Titulares de los Datos Personales Volúmen 4. Procedimientos de Datos Personales ante el INAI' pp. 31–32, available at: https://home.inai.org.mx/wp-content/documentos/GuiasTitulares/Guia%20Titulares-04_PDF.pdf.

In the event that the cited infractions persist repeatedly, an additional fine may be imposed that will range from 100 to 320,000 days of the minimum wage in force in Mexico City (currently the daily value of the UMA). Concerning penalties dealing with the processing of sensitive data, the sanctions may be increased by up to a double of the established amounts.

270. The Tax Administration Service agency is responsible for the execution of the sanctions, once the resolution of INAI is final. In other words, the data controller should not have challenged INAI's resolution or that the procedure, through which the INAI's resolution was challenged, has been completed before the judicial authority.

271. Complainants who believe that they have suffered damage or injury to their property or rights, as a result of non-compliance with the LFPDPPP, its Regulation and other applicable regulations may exercise the rights they deem convenient for the purposes of obtaining an appropriate compensation or redress, in terms of the applicable law. This does not imply that the complainants can obtain any economic benefit from the sanctions established by the INAI.

272. In accordance with the INAI's annual work reports, the highest number of fines imposed on data controllers and individuals that infringed the FLPPDPPP and its Regulation were in the period from October 2018 to September 2019. During this period, fines amounted to a total of MXN 112,397,139.25 (EUR 4,683,741). In contrast, in the period from October 2019 to September 2020, the total amount of fines was only MXN 56,771,662.6 (EUR 2,365,752).[93]

273. Additionally, INAI reports a total amount of fines of MXN 39,324,000 (EUR 1,675,000) from January to November 2020 imposed on data controllers and individuals that infringed the FLPPDPPP and its Regulation. According to INAI, during the last period of time, the sectors most commonly sanctioned are business support services and waste management & remediation services, followed by construction, professional, scientific and technical services, and financial and insurance services. Among the most frequent conducts that are subject to sanctions are: (i) the processing of personal data in contravention of the principles set forth in the LFPDPPP and its Regulation; (ii) collecting or transferring personal information without the consent of the data subject; (iii) obstructing acts of verification of the authority; (iv) omit one or more requirements in the privacy notice; and (v) the incorrect processing of sensitive data.[94]

93. Cfr. INAI, Activity Prepared Reports submitted to the Senate of the Mexican Union Congress. Available at: https://micrositios.inai.org.mx/informesinai/. The difference in the amounts of fines can be explained by the suspension of proceedings due to the COVID-19 pandemic.

94. INAI, 'Multas impuestas en 2020 por Infracciones a la Ley Federal de Protección de Datos Personales suman más de 39 MDP'. INAI. Comunicado INAI/011/21, Ciudad de México, 10 de enero de 2021, available at: https://home.inai.org.mx/wp-content/documentos/SalaDePrensa/Comunicados/Comunicado%20INAI-011-21.pdf.

Part IX. Specific Processing Situations

Chapter 1. Processing for Journalistic Purposes and Academic, Artistic or Literary Expression

274. Unlike Article 85 of the GDPR that provides the reconciliation of the right to personal data with the right to freedom of expression and information including processing for journalistic purposes and the purposes of academic, artistic or literary expression and the exemption and derogations, the LFPDPPP and its Regulation do not have a similar or equivalent provision.

Chapter 2. Processing of Personal Information Versus Public Access to Official Documents

275. The LFPDPPP and its Regulation do not have a provision similar or equivalent to Article 86 of the GDPR that allows to reconcile public access to official documents with the right to the protection of personal data for tasks conducted in the public interest.

276. Concerning access to information to public and official documents of government agencies, there are two main laws in Mexico that govern access to information to entities from the public sector.

277. First, the Federal Law of Transparency and Access to Public Information (FLTAPI). The main purpose of this law is to guarantee the right of access to public information held by any authority, entity, organization and body of the Legislative, Executive and Judicial branches, autonomous entities, political parties, trusts and public funds, as well as any natural or legal person or union that receives and uses federal public resources or conducts acts of authority under the terms provided by the Federal Constitution and the General Law of Transparency and Access to Public Information (GLTAPI).[95]

278. Second, the GLTAPI. The purpose of the GLTAPI is to establish the principles, general grounds and procedures to guarantee the right of access to information held by any authority, entity, organization and body of the Legislative, Executive and Judicial powers, autonomous bodies, political parties, trusts and public funds, as well as of any individual, legal person or union that receives and uses public resources or conduct acts of authority of the Federation, of the States and the Municipalities in Mexico.[96]

The GLTAPI establishes the National System of Transparency, Access to Public Information and Protection of Personal Data. The main purpose of the national system is to coordinate and evaluate the actions related to transversal public policies on transparency, access to information and protection of personal data, as well as to establish and implement the criteria and guidelines in accordance with the provisions of the GLTAPI and other applicable regulations.

279. The following entities are part of the National System of Transparency, Access to Public Information and Protection of Personal Data:

(i) INAI;
(ii) national and state agencies specialized in access to information;
(iii) the Auditing Superior Authority of the Federation;

95. The Federal Law of Transparency and Access to Public Information (FLTAPI) is available at: http://www.diputados.gob.mx/LeyesBiblio/pdf/LFTAIP_270117.pdf.
96. The General Law of Transparency and Access to Public Information (GLTAPI) is available at: http://www.diputados.gob.mx/LeyesBiblio/pdf/LGTAIP_130820.pdf.

(iv) the General Archive of the Nation; and
(v) the National Institute of Statistics, Geography and Informatics (INEGI).

The main functions and activities of the National System are established in Article 31 of the GLTAPI.[97]

Further, the GLTAPI establishes a National Council pertaining to the National System of Transparency, Access to Information and Data Protection provided under Articles 32–36 of the GLTAPI. The National Council is composed of the main heads of the agencies specialized in access to information and data protection, or a Commissioner appointed by the Plenary and it is chaired by the President of INAI.

97. The website of the National System of Transparency, Access to Public Information and Protection of Personal Data is available at: http://www.snt.org.mx/

Chapter 3. Processing of the National Identification Number

280. The LFPDPPP and its Regulation do not contain a similar or equivalent provision to Article 87 of the GDPR concerning specific conditions for the processing of national identification numbers or any other identifier of general application.

281. The national official identity documents for Mexicans are the Voting Card and the Voting Card Abroad ('Credencial para Votar' y 'Credencial para Votar en el Extranjero'). The National Electoral Institute (INE) is the federal agency responsible for the issuance of these documents. All the personal information that Mexican citizens provide to INE in order to obtain these identity cards is protected under the following laws and regulations:

- FLTAPI.
- GLTAPI.
- GLPPDPGPSI.
- Regulation of the INE on Protection of Personal Data.
- General Guidelines for Access, Rectification, Cancellation and Opposition to Personal Data which are part of INE's Electoral List.
- General Guidelines for Document and Information Requests made under Article 126 section 3 of the General Law of Institutions and Electoral Proceedings.
- General Guidelines for the access, verification and disclosure of personal data in possession of the Executive Direction of the Federal Electoral Registry by the members of the General, Local and District Councils, the Oversight Commissions of the Federal Register of Voters and the Local Public Bodies.
- Agreement of the General Council of the INE, by which the implementation of the verification service of the data of the Voting Card is approved, which will serve to safeguard the right to data protection of citizens contained in the Electoral Register.

282. The website of INE contains a privacy policy that describes how said federal agency processes personal data of citizens, how it conducts data transfers. The privacy policy includes an address for the exercise of ARCO rights, and a description of the applicable regulations for the collection and processing of personal information that is incorporated into the National Electoral Registry.[98]

98. The privacy policy of INE's Federal Electoral Registry is available at: https://www.ine.mx/credencial/manifestacion-proteccion-datos-personales-del-registro-federal-electores/.

Chapter 4. Processing in the Context of Employment

283. The LFPDPPP and its Regulation do not contain a provision equivalent or similar to Article 88 of the GDPR concerning the processing of personal data in the employment context.

284. The LFPDPPP and its Regulation are applicable if the employer is a private entity or organization that collects and processes personal information of individuals in national territory. For instance, job recruiting agencies and companies are regulated by the LFPDPPP and its Regulation if they collect and process information of data subjects for purposes of employment.

285. If the employer is a federal, state, government agency, entity or organization, the applicable law to the processing of personal information for purposes of employment is the GLPPDPGPSI.

Chapter 5. Processing for Scientific Research, Public Archiving and Statistical Purposes

286. Unlike Article 89 of the GDPR that provides specific derogations and the use of appropriate safeguards for processing for archiving purposes in the public interest, scientific or historical research or statistical purposes, the LFPDPPP and its Regulation do not have a similar or equivalent provision.

§1. Archiving

287. The *General Archives Law* published on 15 June 2018 is the law that governs public archiving.[99]

The main purpose of *the General Archives Law* is to establish the general principles and grounds for the organization and conservation, administration and homogeneous preservation of archives in possession of any authority, entity, organism of the Legislative, Executive and Judicial powers, autonomous bodies, political parties, trusts and public funds, as well as any individual, legal entity or union that receives and spends public resources or conducts acts of authority of the Federation, of states and the municipalities.

288. This law also determines the bases of organization and operation of the National Archives System and promotes the safeguarding, dissemination and public access of private archives of historical, social, cultural, scientific and technical relevance of the Nation.

289. The General Archives Law establishes as an obligation that the obliged parties establish in their annual programme the procedures for the generation, administration, use, control and migration of electronic formats, as well as long-term preservation and conservation plans that provide for the migration, emulation or any other method of preservation and conservation of electronic archival documents, relying on the provisions emanating from the National Council, which is the coordinating institution of the National Archives System. The obliged parties shall implement automated systems for document management and file administration that allow for the registration and control of document management processes.

290. The General Archive is a decentralized non-sectorial entity, with legal personality and own patrimony, with technical and managerial autonomy that has among its responsibilities the implementation and enforcement of the General Archives Law.

99. The General Archives Law is available at: http://www.diputados.gob.mx/LeyesBiblio/pdf/LGA_150618.pdf.

Chapter 6. Processing for Marketing and Advertising

291. Article 30 of the Regulation establishes that among the purposes of processing referred to in Article 16 subsection II of the FLPPDPP shall include those concerning processing for marketing, advertising or commercial exploration, respectively.

This is without detriment to the current governing legal provisions, regulating processing for the purposes set out in the previous paragraph when said provisions provide for a higher protection to the data subject than the ones provided in the FLPPDPP and its Regulation.

§1. Marketing and Advertising Practices for Consumers

292. In the area of consumer protection law, the FCPL establishes specific rules for suppliers and companies, including marketing and advertising companies when they use and send commercial information to consumers via e-mail.

I. Marketing and Advertising Information for Consumers

293. Article 16 of the FCPL provides that suppliers and companies which use information on consumers for marketing or advertising purposes are obliged to inform, free of charge, to any person that so requests, if the supplier or company keeps any information on such person. If such information exists, the supplier or company shall make it available to such person or his representative upon request, as well as to inform on the information shared with third parties, the identity of such third parties and the recommendations conducted by the supplier or company. The answer to each request shall be given within thirty days from the day of the initial request. In the event of any ambiguity or inaccuracy in the information of a consumer, the consumer must notify the supplier or the company, who must make the correction within a term of thirty days from the date of the initial request, the corrections that the consumer indicates, and report the corrections to the third parties to whom the information has been provided.

The second paragraph of Article 16 of the FCPL provides that marketing or advertising purposes should be understood as the offering and promotion of goods, products or services to consumers.

II. Information Disclosures and Opt-Out Clause

294. Article 17 of the FCPL provides that advertising or publicity sent to consumers shall contain the name, address, phone and, in the absence thereof, the e-mail address of the supplier or of the company that sends the advertising or publicity on behalf of the supplier, and the info of Profeco.

The consumer may directly request specific suppliers and companies using consumers information for marketing or advertising purposes not to be contacted in his home, workplace, e-mail address or through any other means in order to offer goods, products or services, as well as not to receive advertising. Further, the consumer may request suppliers and companies using information on consumers for marketing or advertising purposes not to assign or transfer his personal information to third parties at any time, except when such assignment or transfer is determined by a judicial authority.

III. Information Purpose and Public Registry of Consumers for Personal Data

295. Article 18 of the FCPL provides that Profeco may keep a public registry of consumers who do not wish that their information be used for marketing or advertising purposes. Consumers may inform Profeco either in writing or via e-mail of their inclusion request in such registry, which shall be free of charge.

296. Article 18*bis* of the FCPL establishes the prohibition for suppliers and companies as well as their customers to use consumers' information for different purposes than those related to marketing or advertising, as well as sending advertising to consumers who expressly requested not to receive it or who are registered in the registry mentioned in Article 18 of the FCPL. Suppliers shall be jointly responsible for managing the information of consumers when such advertising is sent through third parties.

Part X. Specific Data Protection Regimes

Chapter 1. Obligations of Professional Secrecy (Including Equivalent Obligations of Secrecy)

297. The LFPDPPP and its Regulation do not have a similar or equivalent provision to Article 90 of the GDPR that establishes obligations of professional secrecy to reconcile the right of protection of personal data. Professional secrecy in Mexico is regulated in the following laws:

- Regulatory Law of Article 5 of the Constitution pertaining to the exercise of professions in Mexico City.
- The Federal Civil Code.
- The Federal Code of Civil Procedure (FCCP).

298. Article 36 of the Regulatory Law of Article 5 of the Constitution pertaining to the exercise of the professions in Mexico City establishes that '*every professional is obliged to strictly maintain the secrecy of the matters entrusted to by his clients, except for the information established mandatorily by the respective laws*'.

299. Article 2590 of the Federal Civil Code punishes the conduct of the solicitor or lawyer who reveals secrets of his client to the opposing party or when the solicitor or lawyer provides him with documents or data that may harm him, making him responsible for all damages and losses. He may also be subject to the criminal liability provided under the Criminal Code.

300. Article 90 of the FCCP establishes that third parties who must maintain professional secrecy are exempt from the obligation to exhibit documents and things in their possession when required to provide assistance to governmental or judicial entities in the enquiries of the truth, in cases where it is a matter of proving against the party to whom they are related.

Chapter 2. Churches and Religious Associations

301. The collection and processing of personal information from religious groups, associations and churches in Mexico are governed by the LFPDPPP and its Regulation. Therefore, all the obligations set forth in the LFPDPPP and its Regulation are compulsory to religious groups and associations duly established in Mexico.

Chapter 3. Law Enforcement Agencies

302. The collection and processing of personal data by law enforcement agencies, including police forces, public prosecutors and public defenders, are governed by the GLPPDPGPSI. This law specifically regulates the collection, use and processing of personal information exclusively in possession of government and public sector entities, including national law enforcement agencies like the Attorney General Office (Fiscalía General de la República) and the National Police (Guardia Nacional).

§1. Government Surveillance

303. Government surveillance in Mexico has received extensive coverage in the international media and press.[100] A large group of national journalists, lawyers, academics, human rights activists and even the members of the Interdisciplinary Group of Independent Experts, a specialized group tasked with investigating the disappearance of forty-three students from a small town known as 'Ayotzinapa' in the State of Guerrero, have been the target of unlawful government surveillance through their mobile devices.

Government surveillance has been documented by a group of Mexican NGOs, R3D, Article 19 Office for Mexico and Central America and SocialTic.[101]

304. R3D claims that at least three national intelligence agencies in Mexico, the *Ministry of Defense (Secretaría de la Defensa),* the former Office of the Attorney General (PGR), *now* Fiscalía General de la República (FGR) and the National Center for Investigation and National Security (CISEN), have acquired the malicious software PEGASUS from NSO Group, a company from Israel which exclusively sells its software to government and intelligence agencies to counter organized criminal activities and terrorism. According to R3D, more than twenty-two journalists and activists were the target of infection with the software PEGASUS across Mexico. In the opinion of R3D, the targeted infections are a clear violation of fundamental human rights under the Mexican Constitution, including the right to privacy, data protection and freedom of expression, and in violation of the international

---

100. *See* New York Times in Spanish, 'Somos los nuevos enemigos del Estado: el espionaje a activistas y periodistas en México', 19 Jun. 2017, available at: https://www.nytimes.com/es/2017/06/19/mexico-pegasus-nso-group-espionaje/ and El País, 'El Gobierno mexicano declaró secretos los contratos sobre el 'software' del espionaje a periodistas', 21 Jun. 2017, available at: https://elpais.com/internacional/2017/06/20/mexico/1497984473_017962.html.

101. *See* Artículo 19, R3D and SOCIAL TIC, 'Gobierno Espía. Vigilancia Sistemática a periodistas y defensores de derechos humanos en México', June 2017, available at: https://articulo19.org/wp-content/uploads/2017/06/Reporte-Gobierno-Espi%CC%81a-Final.pdf.

See also Red en Defensa de los Derechos Digitales (R3D), 'El Estado de la Vigilancia. Fuera de Control', November 2016, available at: https://r3d.mx/wp-content/uploads/R3D-edovigilancia2016.pdf. This report analyses the applicable regulation in Mexico and the current state of practice of government surveillance of law enforcement and investigative agencies and advocates for measures that seek to prevent the use of general surveillance measures and its impunity in Mexico.

human right principles of necessity and proportionality with respect to the surveillance capabilities of the aforementioned national intelligence agencies.[102]

305. On 16 June 2017, the targeted surveillance victims through R3D filed a criminal complaint before the former PGR (now FGR) in order for that agency to investigate and prosecute the possible commission of the crime of communication surveillance under the Criminal Code. However, the criminal investigation has not yet been fully resolved.

306. On 23 November 2018, INAI approved the initiation of a verification procedure against the now extinct PGR (now FGR) related to the acquisition of the software PEGASUS. After the completion of the Verification Procedure, INAI determined that the FGR failed to comply with the principles of security and accountability provided under the GLPPDPGPSI.[103]

307. On 20 February 2019, INAI granted a hearing to the Internal Control Unit of the FGR in order to determine whether the public officials in charge of operating the software PEGASUS incurred in administrative responsibilities. Subsequently, the Plenary of INAI instructed the FGR *inter alia* to implement the following measures:

- Accredit, in a formal manner, that the PEGASUS software had been uninstalled from the Unit for Cybercrime Investigations and Operations of the Criminal Investigation Agency and any other equipment in possession of the FGR.
- Specify the policies, methods and techniques accounting for the uninstallation of the software, considering the irreversibility, security and confidentiality; as well as convincingly prove that it is no longer feasible to reinstal the software acquired in a computer in possession of the FGR.[104]

INAI's judgment seeks to help clarify the irregularities detected in the use of the software PEGASUS by the former PGR officials against journalists, activists and academics, as well as to dissuade and prevent any form of future intervention of private communications without meeting the legal requirements established under the national legislation.

308. Unfortunately, said actions have not prevented national law enforcement authorities from acquiring surveillance technologies on behalf of national security. According to a press release of the Spanish newspaper El País of April 2021, the

102. For further info on the operation and surveillance capabilities of the Software Pegasus in Mexico, *see* Artículo 19, R3D and SOCIAL TIC, 'Gobierno Espía. Vigilancia Sistemática a periodistas y defensores de derechos humanos en México', *supra* note 95, pp. 5–7.
103. For a detailed background on the investigation procedure launched by INAI, *see*: Blanca Lilia Ibarra Cadena, 'México No Necesita un Gobierno Espía', La Silla Rota, 25 Feb. 2019, available at: https://goo.gl/jSXBXj.
104. INAI. Comunicado del INAI/054/19 of 20 Feb. 2019, 'Determina INAI que FGR incumplió la Ley General de Protección de Datos Personales en Posesión de Sujetos Obligados', available at: http://inicio.ifai.org.mx/Comunicados/Comunicado%20INAI-054-19.pdf.

FGR has acquired intelligence programmes for the geolocation of mobile phones and for the analysis of large amounts of data during the current administration of AMLO. Between 2019 and 2020, the FGR signed at least four contracts for the amount of USD 5.6 million with the company Neolinx de México.

309. According to El País, the purchases were made under a secret heading on national security expenses; therefore, the contracts of FGR were not subject to transparency requirements. The NGO, R3D considers that the execution of this type of intelligence programmes may violate human rights because in some cases, it could lead to unauthorized massive surveillance that contravenes the legal principles of necessity, proportionality and judicial authorization.[105]

105. For further information on surveillance equipment programs entered by the FGN, *see* El Pais, 'La Fiscalía de México ha contratado en los dos últimos años programas para el espionaje masivo de teléfonos móviles', 14 Apr. 2021, available at: https://elpais.com/mexico/2021-04-14/la-fiscalia-de-mexico-ha-contratado-en-los-dos-ultimos-anos-programas-para-el-espionaje-masivo-de-telefonos-moviles.html.

Chapter 4. National Security Services

310. Mexico has a National Security Law in force since 31 January 2005. The main purpose of this law is to establish the grounds of integration and coordinated action of the institutions and authorities in charge of preserving national security, in their respective areas of competence.

The National Security Law also establishes the form and terms in which the authorities of the state entities and municipalities shall collaborate with the Federation in matters of national security and regulates the legitimate instruments to strengthen the controls applicable to the subject matter.[106]

311. Pursuant to Article 3 of the National Security Law, 'National Security' is defined as 'the immediate and direct actions aimed to maintain the integrity, stability and permanence of the Mexican State, which lead to:

(i) the protection of the Mexican nation against threats and risks that the country faces;
(ii) the preservation of national sovereignty and independence and the defence of the territory;
(iii) the maintenance of the constitutional order and the strengthening of government democratic institutions;
(iv) the maintenance of the unity of the integral parts of the Federation referred to in Article 43 of the Federal Constitution;
(v) the legitimate defence of the Mexican State with respect to other States or entities of international law; and
(vi) the preservation of democracy, founded on the economic, social and political development of the country and its inhabitants'.

312. Article 4 establishes that national security will be governed by the principles of legality, responsibility, respect for the fundamental rights of protection of the human person and individual and civil and social liberties, confidentiality, loyalty, transparency, efficiency, coordination and cooperation.

313. The Security Council is the body in charge of establishing and executing national security policy. It is composed of the President of the Republic, the Interior Ministry, and the heads of the main secretaries of the State.

314. Article 8 section V of the National Security Law establishes that in relation to information pertaining national security, the provisions of the Federal Law on Transparency and Access to Public Government Information (FLTAPGI) shall apply.

106. The National Security Law is available at: http://www.diputados.gob.mx/LeyesBiblio/pdf/LSegNac_181220.pdf.

315. The National Security Law establishes the CISEN, as a decentralized administrative body of the Ministry of the Interior, with technical, operational and spending autonomy, directly attached to the head of the Ministry of the Interior. Among the main attributions of the CISEN are:

(i) execute intelligence tasks as part of the national security system that contribute to the preservation of the integrity, stability and permanence of the Mexican State, to support governance and to strengthen the rule of law;
(ii) process the information generated by its operations, determine its trend, value, meaning and specific interpretation and formulate the conclusions deriving from the respective assessments, with the purpose of safeguarding the security of the country.

The National Security Law contains a chapter on information and intelligence (Articles 29–32) that establishes the form of how the information shall be collected and processed for national security purposes.

316. Article 29 provides that intelligence shall be interpreted as 'the knowledge obtained from the collection, processing, dissemination and exploitation of information, for decision-making in matters of National Security'.

317. Article 30 establishes that information may only be collected, compiled, processed and disseminated for national security purposes by the authorized entities.

318. Article 31 provides that in the exercise of intelligence powers, the parties will enjoy technical autonomy and may make use of any information gathering method, without affecting civil liberties or human rights.

319. Article 32 establishes a definition on counterintelligence, which is defined as 'the protection measures of the instances against harmful acts, as well as the actions aimed at dissuading or counteracting their commission'.

320. The National Security Law contains a chapter on intervention of communications, and establishes a specific procedure to conduct it.

§1. Application

321. Article 34 establishes that the CISEN pursuant to the ninth paragraph of Article 16 of the Federal Constitution may request, in the terms and conditions provided in the National Security Law, judicial authorization to conduct the intervention of private communications in the field of national security.

322. Article 35 establishes that communications intervention should be understood as 'the taking, listening, monitoring, recording or search of private communications of any kind and by any means, device or technology conducted by an authorized instance'.

Pursuant to the second paragraph of Article 35, the Judicial Branch of the Federation, in accordance with its internal law, will determine the national courts that may hear the requests to intervene private communications that are presented in matters of national security.

323. Pursuant to Article 36, the judicial procedures that are established to authorize the requests for intervention in matters of national security shall not be contentious in nature, and their procedural records will lack evidence value in judicial or administrative procedures.

When the CISEN cooperates in the prevention of justice activities, the intervention of private communications where technical assistance is provided will have a different nature and shall adjust to the requirements and formalities established in the National Code of Criminal Procedure and the Federal Law on Organized Crime.

§2. PROCEDURE

324. Pursuant to Article 37 of the National Security Law, the procedure is confidential; therefore, the requests shall be kept in a special government book that will be managed by the staff appointed for this purpose by the judge. Access to the files will not be allowed to any person, except the Court's secretary and the person authorized in writing by the General Director of the CISEN.

325. Article 38 establishes the requirements that the application request shall contain. Among said requirements are the following:

(i) A detailed description of the facts and situations that represent a threat to National Security in the terms of Article 5 of the National Security Law. The description must not include identification data of individuals, places or things which when undue disseminated may put their safety at risk or of the ongoing investigation. The file formed for this reason will be handled in secrecy and will be kept in the secrecy of the Court.
(ii) The considerations that motivated the request.
(iii) The period of validity of the authorization that is requested.

326. Article 39 of the National Security Law establishes that the judge must provide acknowledgement of receipt and issue within twenty-four hours from the request, a well-founded and motivated resolution in which he can grant or deny the requested authorization. In case of denying it, the judge will indicate the reasons for its refusal and the additional requirements that must be met.

The intervention may be applied to private communications and broadcasts, conducted by any means of transmission, known or to be known, or between present parties, including the recording of private images.

327. Article 41 establishes that the control and execution of intervention of communications in the field of national security are the responsibility of the CISEN. The judge may require periodic reports regarding the execution of the authorization, which at all times must comply with the conditions established in Article 40.

328. Article 42 establishes that the data obtained from the activities authorized by judicial authorization will be considered confidential information. Only the Director General of the CISEN, the persons designated by the Council and the competent federal judges may know this information.

§3. Validity

329. Pursuant to Article 43, intervention of communications will only be authorized for a period not exceeding 180 calendar days. As an exemption on duly justified cases, the judge may authorize an extension up to an equal period of the original authorization.

330. Pursuant to Article 44, the request for an extension will be subject to the procedure referred to in Section II of the National Security Law, and it shall specify the considerations that justify that such intervention continues to be necessary to investigate a threat to National Security.

§4. Obligations

331. The National Security Law includes obligations for both the judiciary and the companies that provide communications services. Article 45 provides that the staff of the Court referred to in Article 37 is obliged to keep the secrecy of the content of the authorization requests and resolutions, as well as the information generated by their application.

332. Further, Article 46 provides that companies that provide or render any kind of communication services are constrained to grant access privileges and comply with the resolutions that authorize activities that are subject matter of the law.

333. Article 47 provides that all information obtained through activities of intervention of communications is part of the information of the CISEN. The final destination of this information will be determined by the National Security Council. The individuals who participate in the procedures of intervention of communications will be prevented from obtaining or keeping the original or copies of the information obtained through such measures, except the staff instructed to do so by the General Director of the National Security Center.

334. Article 48 establishes that the information and any type of materials that are the result of an intervention of private communications authorized in accordance with Chapter II of the National Security Law shall be considered confidential. The unauthorized dissemination of the information will be punished under this law, without detriment to other applicable legal regulations.

§5. Emergency Cases

335. Article 49 of the National Security Law, establishes that, under special circumstances and when complying with the procedure established in Section II of Chapter II, the situation puts at risk the success of an investigation, and when there are indications that a threat to the national security may occur, the judge may immediately authorize the required measure in view of its urgency.

§6. Confidentiality of Information

336. Pursuant to Article 51 of the National Security Law, reserved information for reasons of National Security will be the following:

(i) Information whose application implies the disclosure of standards, procedures, methods, sources, technical specifications, technology or useful equipment for the generation of intelligence for national security, regardless of the nature or origin of the documents that consign it, or
(ii) Information whose disclosure may be used to update or enhance a threat.

§7. Information Whose Disclosure May Be Used to Update or Enhance a Threat

337. Article 54 of the National Security Law establishes that any person who for any reason participates or has knowledge of intelligence products, sources, methods, measures or operations, records or information derived from the actions provided for in the legislation must refrain from disseminating it by any means and adopt the necessary measures to prevent it from being advertised.

338. Article 55 of the National Security Law establishes that the CISEN is responsible for defining and creating protection measures, destruction, security codes in communications and other relevant aspects for the safeguarding of the information generated as a result of the coordination systems in matters of national security.

§8. Protection of the Rights of Individuals

339. Title Five of the National Security Law regulates the protection of rights of individuals in four articles.

340. Article 61 establishes that public servants whose areas are related to national security will guide the performance of their functions based on the principles set forth in Article 3. Public servants shall preserve the principles of legality, responsibility, respect for fundamental rights and individual and civil liberties, confidentiality, loyalty, transparency, efficiency, coordination and cooperation that must be complied with pursuant to the legislation regulating the public service.

341. Article 62 establishes that no person shall be obliged to provide information to public servants of the CISEN outside of the scope and conditions set forth by law.

342. Article 63 establishes that the personal data of individuals who provide information shall be kept confidential.

343. Finally, Article 64 mandates that confidential information shall not be disclosed, despite not having links to threats to national security or through preventive actions or procedures thereof, which injure the privacy, dignity of individuals or reveal personal information.

Chapter 5. Medical and Health Records

344. Medical records and personal data of medical patients are regulated in a secondary regulation, known as the National Official Norm on Medical Records (NOM-004-SSA3-2012) published in DOF on 15 October 2012.[107]

§1. Purpose

345. Pursuant to section 1, the main purpose of this national official norm is to set forth the obligatory scientific, ethical, technical and administrative criteria for the elaboration, integration, use, management, filing, preservation, ownership, and the confidentiality of personal medical records.

§2. Scope of Application

346. The national official norm is compulsory for personnel and staff of the health sector and medical and health service providers from the public, social and private sectors, including private medical offices and practices.

§3. Definitions

347. The National Official Norm on Medical Records contains a list of twelve definitions, which provide further guidelines to obliged parties in the execution of their respective obligations. Among the most relevant definitions are:

- *Medical Records.* A unique set of information and personal data of a patient composed within any type of health care establishment, whether pubic, social or private, which is composed of written documents, graphs, images, electronic, magnetic, optical documents and of any other kind through which health staff will include registries, annotations, and where applicable the respective certifications of the medical attention and intervention of a patient consistent with the legal governing provisions.
- *Clinical History.* A document drafted by a doctor, which registers the relevant aspects of the medical attention of a patient contained in his medical record.

§4. Main Obligations

348. Section 5 of the National Official Norm on Medical Records provides that all health providers from the public, social or private sector are obliged to integrate and preserve medical records. The staff of health service providers is jointly and

107. The National Official Norm on Medical Records (NOM-004-SSA3-2012) is available at: http://www.dof.gob.mx/nota_detalle.php?codigo=5272787&fecha=15/10/2012.

severally liable concerning this obligation regardless of the form that said staff was hired.

349. Pursuant to section 5.5.1, the data provided to medical staff by the patient or a third party shall be kept confidential in accordance with the professional health secret and other applicable legal provisions. The disclosure of data to third parties may only be made through a written request of the patient, the legal guardian, the legal representative or a doctor duly authorized by his patient, legal guardian or legal representative.

350. Other relevant obligations of health professionals under the National Official Norm on Medical Records are the following:

(i) Disclose information to the patient or the legal guardian, legal representative, family members and competent authorities, which includes judicial authorities, criminal justice authorities and administrative authorities. Health medical records need to be requested in writing.
(ii) Manage health records with discretion and confidentiality following the scientific and ethical principles governing medical practice, the provisions contained in the National Official Norm on Medical Records and other applicable laws.
(iii) Complete all medical notes and reports with full and complete information of the patient, age and gender, as well as the date, time and full name of the person drafting the medical note and the handwritten or electronic or digital signature, where applicable.
(iv) State the use of electronic, optical, magnetic, electromagnetic or any other technologies in the incorporation of a medical record in accordance with the applicable legislation.
(v) Integrate the medical record according to the generic services of general consultation, speciality, emergency and hospitalization. In addition, the clinical record shall include the requirements provided in sections 3.2, 3.3, 3.5, 3.7, 3.8, 3.9, 3.11, 3.13, 3.14, 3.15 and 3.16 of the official norm. When several services are provided in the same establishment for medical care, a single clinical file must be integrated for each patient, containing each and every document generated by the staff involved in the attention of the patient.

§5. Preservation Term

351. Pursuant to the first paragraph of section 5.4, medical records are owned by the institution or the provider of medical services that generates them, when the latter does not depend on an institution. In the case of public sector institutions, in addition to what is provided in the official norm, they must comply with the laws in force on the matter. Notwithstanding the foregoing, the patient as a provider of information and beneficiary of medical care has ownership rights over the information for the protection of his health, as well as for the protection of the confidentiality of his data, in the terms of this official norm and other applicable laws.

352. The second paragraph of section 5.4. of the National Official Norm on Medical Records provides that the documents and information pertaining to a patient shall be preserved for a minimum term of five years from the date of the last medical record or registration.

The personal data contained in the medical record, which allow for the identification of a patient in terms of the scientific and ethical principles guiding medical practice, shall not be disclosed through any means.

353. Regarding the publication or disclosure of personal data contained in medical records for the purpose of medical research, teaching, photography that allow for the identification of a patient, the written authorization of the patient will always be required, and where applicable, necessary measures shall be adopted so as to prevent the identification of the patient.

354. The official norm establishes the type of information, the form and methodology that different categories of health records shall be conformed and managed. These categories are the following:

(i) General Medical Consultation and Specialty (section 6).
(ii) Medical Notes in Urgencies (section 7).
(iii) Medical Notes and Hospitalization (section 8).
(iv) Reports of the Professional and Technical Staff (section 9).
(v) Informed Consent Letters (section 10).

§6. Oversight

355. The Ministry of Health and the governments of State entities within the scope of their respective competences are responsible for the enforcement of the Official Norm on Medical Records.

The Official Norm on Medical Records includes the technical requirement, documents and other information that different categories of medical records shall contain, such as the following:

(i) Medical records for general and specialization consultations.
(ii) Medical notes in urgencies.
(iii) Medical notes in hospitalization.
(iv) Reports of professional and technical staff.
(v) Letters of informed consent.
(vi) Voluntary exit sheet.
(vii) Public prosecutor notification sheet.
(viii) Report of cause of death subject to epidemiological surveillance.
(ix) Death and foetal death sheet.

Chapter 6. Data Protection for Public Sector Institutions

356. Mexico's Executive Branch issued the GLPPDPGPSI on 26 January 2017.[108] The GLPPDPGPSI contains a total of 168 articles divided into eleven titles and eight transitory provisions. The transitory provisions establish the different dates and phases that this law shall come into full effect.

§1. Purpose of the GLPPDPGPSI

357. Article 1 provides that this law is of public order and of general observance in the whole Mexican Republic. It regulates Article 6 section A and 16, second paragraph, of the Federal Constitution, regarding the protection of personal data in possession of government and public sector entities.

All the provisions of the GLPPDPGPSI are applicable and shall directly be binding upon government entities belonging to the federal order as the case may be, and within the scope of its competence.

INAI shall exercise the powers conferred by the GLPPDPGPSI, irrespective of those granted in other applicable laws and regulations.

The purpose of the GLPPDPGPSI is to establish the baseline, principles and procedures to guarantee the right to the protection of personal data that every person has in possession of government and public sector entities.

Any authority, entity, body and agency of the Executive, Legislative and Judicial branches, autonomous bodies, political parties, trusts and public funds at the federal, state and municipal levels are bound by the GLPPDPGPSI.

Work Unions and any other natural or legal person who receives and exercises public resources or conducts acts of authority at the federal, state and municipal level shall be responsible for personal data, in accordance with the applicable regulations for the protection of personal data held by private parties.

In cases other than those mentioned in the previous paragraph, natural and legal persons shall be subject to the provisions of the Federal Law on the Protection of Personal Data held by Private Parties (FLPPDPP).

§2. Objectives of the GLPPDPGPSI

358. The GLPPDPGPSI sets forth a number of objectives in nine subsections of Article 2. These objectives are as follows:

(i) Distribute powers between guarantor entities of the Federation and the Federative Entities in the matter of protection of personal data in possession of government and public sector entities.

108. The General Law on Protection of Personal Data in Possession of Government and Public Sector Institutions (GLPPDPGPSI) of 26 Jan. 2017 is available at: http://www.dof.gob.mx/nota_detalle.php?codigo=5469949&fecha=26/01/2017 (Last visited March 2019).

(ii) Establish the minimum bases and homogeneous conditions that shall govern the processing of personal data and the exercise of the rights of access, rectification, cancellation and opposition through simple and expeditious procedures.
(iii) Regulate the organization and operation of the *National System of Transparency, Access to Information and Protection of Personal Data* referred to in this law and the General Law on Transparency and Access to Public Information, regarding its functions for the protection of personal data in possession of government and public sector entities.
(iv) Guarantee the observance of the principles of protection of personal data contained in this law and other provisions that are applicable in the subject matter.
(v) Protect personal data in possession of any authority, entity, body and agency of the Executive, Legislative and Judicial powers, autonomous bodies, political parties, trusts and public funds, of the Federation, Federal Entities and municipalities, with the purpose of regulating its due processing.
(vi) Ensure that every individual can exercise the right to the protection of personal data.
(vii) Promote, foster and spread a culture of personal data protection.
(viii) Establish mechanisms to ensure compliance with and effective application of appropriate enforcement measures for those conducts that overlap with the provisions of this law.
(ix) Regulate the means for challenging resolutions and procedures for the filing of unconstitutional actions and constitutional controversies by local guarantor agencies and of the Federation in accordance with their respective powers.

§3. Definitions

359. Article 3 of the GLPPDPGPSI contains a list of thirty-four definitions, the main purpose of which is to clarify their exact meaning within the scope of application and interpretation of this law. Among the definitions are: privacy notice, databases, blocking, cloud computing, consent, personal data, sensitive personal data, ARCO rights, dissociation, security document, data protection impact assessments, public access source, security measures, administrative security measures, physical security measures, technical security measures, national programme of protection of personal data, data transfer, data processing and transparency unit, among others.

§4. Scope of Application

360. Article 4 of the GLPPDPGPSI is applicable to any processing of personal data on physical or electronic media, regardless of the form or modality of its creation, type of support, processing, storage and organization.

§5. Public Access Sources

361. Article 5 of the GLPPDPGPSI sets forth a list of criteria considered as sources of public access. These are the following: (i) Internet websites or remote or local electronic, optical and other technology media, provided that the website where the personal data is located is designed to provide information to the public and is open for general consultation; (ii) telephone directories in terms of specific regulations; (iii) official newspapers, gazettes or bulletins, in accordance with its regulations; (iv) social media, and (v) public records according to the corresponding applicable provisions. The last paragraph of this article provides that a source of public access will not be considered as such when the information contained therein is or has an unlawful origin.

§6. Limits and Exceptions to Data Protection

362. Article 6 of the GLPPDPGPSI establishes that the State shall guarantee the privacy of individuals and shall ensure that third parties do not engage in conduct that may affect this right arbitrarily.

The right to the protection of personal data shall only be restricted for reasons of national security, in terms of the law on the subject, provisions of public order, public safety and health or to protect the rights of third parties.

§7. Sensitive and Children Data

363. Pursuant to Article 7 of the GLPPDPGPSI, as a general rule, sensitive personal data may not be processed unless the data subject has given his expressed consent or otherwise, under the criteria listed in Article 22 of the GLPPDPGPSI. The second paragraph of this article establishes that in the processing of personal data of minors, the best interests of the child or teenager should prevail, in terms of the applicable laws.

§8. Interpretation of the Law

364. Article 8 of the GLPPDPGPSI provides that the application and interpretation of this Law shall be conducted in accordance with the provisions of the Federal Constitution, the international treaties that the Mexican State is a party, as well as the binding resolutions and decisions issued by the national and international specialized bodies, favouring the right to privacy, the protection of personal data and the broadest protection to individuals at all times.

For purposes of interpretation, the criteria, determinations and opinions of the national and international bodies on the protection of personal data may be taken into account.

§9. Laws of Supplementary Application

365. Article 9 of the GLPPDPGPSI establishes that in the absence of express provisions in this law, the provisions of the FCCP and of the Federal Law on Administrative Procedure shall apply supplementarily. The laws of the Federative Entities, within the scope of their respective powers, shall determine the provisions that are applicable to them in a supplementary matter to the data protection authority in the application and interpretation of this Law.

§10. The National System on Transparency, Access to Information and Protection of Personal Data

366. Articles 10–15 of the GLPPDPGPSI set forth the attributions, objectives and activities of the *National System on Transparency, Access to Information and Protection of Personal Data*, the main purpose of which is to coordinate and evaluate activities related to transversal public policies on the protection of personal data, as well as the establishment and implementation of criteria and guidelines on the subject matter pursuant to said law and the *General Law on Transparency and Access to Public Government Information.*

367. In accordance with Article 11, the *National System on Transparency, Access to Information and Protection of Personal Data* shall contribute to maintain the full validity of the right to the protection of personal data at the national level in all three levels of government.

This joint and integral effort will contribute to the implementation of public policies with strict adherence to the applicable normativity in the matter; the full exercise and respect of the right to the protection of personal data and the dissemination of a culture of this right and its accessibility.

368. Pursuant to Article 12, the *National System on Transparency, Access to Information and Protection of Personal Data* has as a principal objective the design, implementation and assessment of a National Programme for the Protection of Personal Data that defines public policy and establishes, as a minimum, objectives, strategies, actions and goals in order to:

(i) promote education and a culture of personal data protection among Mexican society;
(ii) foster the exercise of rights of access, rectification, cancellation and opposition;
(iii) train the obligated entities in matters of protection of personal data;
(iv) promote the implementation and maintenance of a security management system as referred to in Article 34 of this law, as well as to promote the adoption of national and international standards and good practices in this area; and
(v) facilitate mechanisms that allow for the measurement, reporting and verification of the established goals.

369. The National Programme for the Protection of Personal Data shall be established as a guiding instrument for the integration and coordination of the *National System on Transparency, Access to Information and Protection of Personal Data*, and shall determine and prioritize the objectives and goals to be met, as well as the definition of the necessary general lines of action.

The National Programme for the Protection of Personal Data shall be evaluated and updated at the end of each year and shall define the set of activities and projects to be carried out during the following year.

370. Pursuant to Article 13, the *National System on Transparency, Access to Information and Protection of Personal Data* will have a National Council. The integration, organization, operation and attributions of the National Council will be conducted in accordance with the GLTAPI and other applicable legislations.

I. Functions of the National System on Transparency, Access to Information and Protection of Personal Data

371. In accordance with Article 14 of the GLPPDPGPSI, the *National System on Transparency, Access to Information and Protection of Personal Data*, in addition to the provisions of the General Law on Transparency and Access to Public Information and other applicable regulations, will have the following functions related to the protection of personal data protection:

(i) Promote the exercise of the right to the protection of personal data throughout the Mexican Republic.
(ii) Foster a culture of protection of personal data among the population.
(iii) Analyse, offer opinions and propose to the bodies authorized to do so projects for reform or modification of regulations in this area.
(iv) Agree and establish coordination mechanisms that allow for the formulation and execution of public instruments and comprehensive, systematic, continuous and evaluable public policies, aimed at fulfilling the objectives and purposes of the National System, of the GLPPDPGPSI and other provisions that may be applicable to the subject matter.
(v) Issue agreements and general resolutions for the operation of the National System.
(vi) Draft, establish and execute general policies on the protection of personal data.
(vii) Promote the effective coordination of the bodies that integrate the National System and to follow up the actions that for that purpose are established.
(viii) Promote the homologation and development of the procedures provided for in this Law and evaluate its progress.
(ix) Design and implement policies on the protection of personal data.
(x) Establish effective mechanisms in order for the society to participate in the evaluation processes of the policies and institutions that are part of the National System.

(xi) Develop common projects of national scope to measure compliance and progress of the responsible entities.
(xii) Enter into collaboration agreements whose purpose is to contribute to the fulfilment of the objectives of the National System and those provided for under the GLPPDPGPSI and other provisions that may be applicable in the matter.
(xiii) Promote and implement actions to guarantee accessibility conditions so that vulnerable groups can exercise, under equal circumstances, their right to the protection of personal data.
(xiv) Propose codes of good practice or models for the protection of personal data.
(xv) Promote communication and coordination with national, federal, state, municipal, authorities and international agencies, with the purpose of promoting the objectives of the GLPPDPGPSI.
(xvi) Propose actions to link the National System with other national, regional or local systems and programmes.
(xvii) Promote and foster the exercise and protection of the right to the protection of personal data, through the implementation, organization and operation of the National Platform, referred to in the General Law on Transparency and Access to Public Information and other applicable regulations.
(xviii) Approve the National Programme for the Protection of Personal Data referred to in Article 12 of the GLPPDPGPSI.
(xix) Issue additional criteria to determine the cases in which there is an intensive or relevant processing of personal data, in accordance with the provisions of Articles 70 and 71 of this Law.
(xx) Issue the necessary administrative provisions for the assessment of the content submitted by the obliged entities in the Impact Assessment in the protection of personal data, in order to issue the corresponding non-binding recommendations.
(xxi) Others that are established in other provisions in the matter for the operation of the National System.

372. Pursuant to Article 15 of the GLPPDPGPSI, the National Council shall operate in accordance with the provisions of the General Law on Transparency and Access to Public Information and other applicable laws.

§11. Principles and Obligations

373. Title Second, Chapter I of the GLPPDPGPSI consisting of Articles 16–30 sets forth the general data protection principles to be observed by the responsible entities. Article 16 establishes that said responsible entities shall observe the principles of lawfulness, purpose, loyalty, consent, quality, proportionality, information and accountability in the processing of personal data.

374. Article 18 stipulates that any processing of personal data carried out by the responsible entity must be justified by specific, legitimate, explicit purposes, related to the attributions that the applicable legislation confers on them. The responsible entity may process personal data for purposes other than those set forth in the privacy notice, provided that it has attributions conferred by law and the consent of the data subject has been given, unless it is a person reported as missing, under the terms provided under this law and other provisions that are applicable to the matter.

375. Article 19 establishes that the responsible entity shall not obtain and process personal data, through deceptive or fraudulent means, privileging the protection of the interests of the data subject and the reasonable expectation of privacy.

I. Consent

376. Article 20 stipulates the form that the consent from the data subject shall be obtained for the processing of personal data by responsible entities. Said consent shall be:

(i) free: without error, bad faith, violence or fraud that may affect the manifestation of the data subject's will;
(ii) specific: referring to concrete, lawful, explicit and legitimate purposes that justify the processing; and
(iii) informed: that the data subject has knowledge of the privacy notice prior to the processing that his personal data shall be subject to.

377. When obtaining the consent of minors or persons who are in a state of interdiction or incapacity declared in accordance with the law, it will be in accordance with the rules of representation provided for in the applicable civil legislation.

378. Article 21 establishes the different forms to express consent. As a general rule, consent may be provided in express or tacit form. Expressed consent is expressed when the will of the data subject is expressed verbally, in writing or by electronic means or any other technology.

Tacit consent is considered as such when the privacy notice has been acknowledged to the data subject, and he does not oppose his will otherwise.

379. As a general rule, tacit consent is considered to be valid, unless the law or applicable provisions require that the will of the data subject shall be expressly granted.

In the case of sensitive personal data, the entity responsible must obtain the express written consent of the data subject for processing, through his handwritten signature, electronic signature or any authentication mechanism established for this purpose, except in the cases provided for under Article 22 of the GLPPDPGPSI.

380. Article 22 sets forth the hypothesis when the entity responsible is not obliged to obtain the consent of the data subject for the processing of his personal data. The hypothesis scenarios are the following:

(i) When a law so provides, such assumptions being in accordance with the bases, principles and provisions established in this law, in no case, may contravene it.
(ii) When transfers made between responsible entities are about personal data that are used for the exercise of their own powers, compatible or similar for the purpose that motivated the processing of personal data.
(iii) Where there is a well-founded and motivated court order, resolution or mandate of a competent authority.
(iv) For the recognition or defence of rights of the data subject before a competent authority.
(v) When personal data are required to exercise a right or comply with obligations arising from a legal relationship between the data subject and the responsible entity.
(vi) When an emergency situation arises that may potentially harm an individual or his property.
(vii) When the personal data are necessary to conduct a treatment for the prevention, diagnosis and the provision of health care.
(viii) When the personal data are available in sources of public access.
(ix) When personal data are subject to a previous disassociation procedure.
(x) When the data subject is a person reported as disappeared under the terms of the law regulating the matter.

II. Quality

381. Article 23 establishes that the responsible entity shall adopt necessary measures to keep personal data accurate, complete, correct and updated so as not to modify the veracity of said data.

When the personal data are no longer necessary for the purpose provided in the privacy notice, they shall be deleted through a blocking procedure and once the conservation term has concluded. The conservation term shall not exceed those for the fulfilment of the purpose that justifies the processing and shall take into account the administrative, accounting, fiscal, legal and historical aspects of personal data.

382. Article 24 establishes the obligation for responsible entities to document the procedures for conservation, blocking and deletion of personal data, which shall include mechanisms that allow to comply with the terms for the deletion of data, as well as to conduct a periodic revision on the need to preserve personal data.

III. Purpose

383. Article 25 provides that responsible entities shall only process personal data that is relevant and strictly necessary for the purpose that justifies its processing.

IV. Information

384. Article 26 stipulates that responsible entities shall inform data subjects through the privacy notice on the existing and main features of the processing of their personal data so that data subjects may take informed decisions.

The second and third paragraph of Article 26 establishes that as general rule, the privacy notice shall be diffused through physical and electronic means and shall be drafted and structured clearly and in a simple way.

The last paragraph of Article 26 provides that when it is not possible to make the privacy notice available to the data subject, directly or in a way or that requires disproportionate efforts, the responsible entity may implement mass communication compensatory measures following the criteria issued by the National Transparency, Access to Public Information and Protection of Personal Data System.

385. Article 27 mandates that the privacy notice shall be acknowledged in two modalities: comprehensive and simplified. This provision enlists in five sections the information that the simplified privacy policy should contain, which shall include the mechanisms and means for the data subject to oppose the processing of his personal data for purposes of data transfers that require the consent of the data subject.

386. Article 28 enlists in seven sections the information and criteria that the comprehensive privacy policy shall contain, which should include the categories of data to be processed, the mechanisms, means and available procedures to exercise ARCO rights, the address of the Transparency Unit and the means through which the responsible entity will inform data subjects on the changes to the privacy notice.

V. Accountability

387. Article 29 stipulates that responsible entities shall implement the mechanisms contained in Article 30 in order to comply with the principles, duties and obligations contained in the law and be accountable to the data subject, INAI and regulatory agencies on the processing of his personal data in its possession, accordingly. Responsible entities shall comply with the Constitution, the international treaties that the Mexican State is a party to and international standards and best practices that do not contradict national legislation.

388. Article 30 establishes that among the mechanisms that responsible entities may take into account in order to comply with the principle of accountability established under the law are at least the following:

(i) To allocate resources authorized for this purpose for the implementation of programmes and policies for the protection of personal data.
(ii) Develop policies and programmes for the protection of personal data, mandatory and enforceable within the organization of responsible entities.
(iii) Implement a programme of training and updating of staff on obligations and other duties in the field of personal data protection.

(iv) Review the policies and programmes of security of personal data periodically in order to determine the modifications that are required.
(v) Establish an internal and/or external monitoring and supervision system, including audits to verify compliance with personal data protection policies.
(vi) Establish procedures to receive and respond to doubts and complaints from data subjects.
(vii) Design, develop and implement its public policies, programmes, services, systems or computer platforms, electronic applications or any other technology involving the processing of personal data, in accordance with the provisions set forth in the law and any other applicable regulation.
(viii) Ensure that its public policies, programmes, services, systems or computer platforms, electronic applications or any other technology involving the processing of personal data by default comply with the obligations set forth in this law and any other applicable regulations.

§12. Obligations

389. Articles 31–42 set forth obligations in the field of information security that need to be implemented and maintained by responsible entities.

I. Security Measures

390. Article 31 mentions that responsible entities shall establish and maintain physical, technical and administrative security measures for the protection of personal data that allow for the protection against damage, loss, modification, destruction, illegal access, use and processing, as well as to guarantee its confidentiality, integrity and availability.

Article 32 stipulates that security measures adopted by responsible parties shall take into consideration the following:

(i) The risk inherent to the personal data processed.
(ii) The sensitivity of the personal data processed.
(iii) The technological development.
(iv) The possible consequences of a data breach to the data subjects.
(v) Conducted transfers of personal data.
(vi) The number of data subjects.
(vii) Previous breaches occurred in processing systems.
(viii) The risk for the potential quantitative or qualitative value that could have the personal data processed for a third person not authorized for possession.

391. Article 33 enlists in eight different sections the activities that responsible entities shall include in the establishment and maintenance of security measures for the protection of personal data.

392. Article 34 mandates that the activities related to the implementation of security measures for the processing of personal data shall be documented and contained in a management system.

393. Article 35 enlists the minimum requirements that the security document shall contain. These requirements are: (i) the inventory of personal data and processing systems; (ii) duties and obligations of persons processing personal data; (iii) the risk analysis; (iv) the breach analysis; (v) the work plan; (vi) mechanisms for monitoring and reviewing security measures; and (vii) the general training programme.

394. Article 36 establishes that responsible entities shall update the security document when the following situations occur: (i) when substantial changes to the processing of personal data result in a change in the level of risk; (ii) as a result of a process of continuous improvement, derived from the monitoring and review of the management system; (iii) as a result of an improvement process to mitigate the impact of a breach of security; and (iv) as a result of implementation of corrective and preventive actions for a security breach.

395. Article 37 stipulates that in the event of a breach of security, the responsible entity should analyse the causes that were presented and implement in its work plan preventive and corrective actions to adapt the security measures and the processing of personal data when this is the case, in order to prevent that the security breach occurs again.

396. Article 38 establishes in four sections what is considered as a security breach in any phase of data processing: (i) unauthorized loss or destruction; (ii) theft, loss or unauthorized copying; (iii) unauthorized use, access or processing; or (iv) unauthorized damage, alteration or modification.

397. Article 39 establishes that the responsible entity shall have a registry of security breaches, which should include date, description, reason and the implementation of corrective actions on an immediate and definitive basis.

398. Article 40 establishes the obligation of responsible entities to inform data subjects without any delay, as well as INAI and supervisory federal entities on the breaches that significantly affect economic or moral rights, once it is confirmed that the breach has occurred and that the entity responsible has begun to take the actions aimed at detonating a process of exhaustive review of the magnitude of the problem, so that the affected data subjects may take the corresponding measures for the defence of their rights.

399. Article 41 stipulates that responsible entities shall inform data subject at least on the following: (i) the nature of the incident; (ii) the compromised personal data; (iii) the recommendations to the data subject on the measures that the data subject may take to protect his interests; (iv) the corrective actions to be immediately conducted; and (v) the means where further information can be obtained.

400. Article 42 mandates that the responsible entity must establish controls or mechanisms that aim at all those who intervene in any phase of the processing of personal data, keep confidentiality regarding such data processing, an obligation that will continue even after the finalization of their relationship. This is without detriment of the articles on access to public information.

§13. Rights of Data Subjects

401. The Third Title of the GLPPDPGPSI which consists of Articles 43–57 establishes the rights of data subjects and its exercise before responsible government entities. Articles 43–56 set forth the terms, conditions to request responsible entities' access, rectification, cancellation and opposition to the processing of personal data and information of data subjects. Article 43 mentions that the exercise of any of the ARCO rights is not a previous requirement, and it does not prevent the exercise of other rights.

402. Article 51 stipulates that responsible entities shall establish easy-to-use procedures that allow for the exercise of ARCO rights, the term of which to provide an answer shall not exceed twenty days from the following day of the reception of the request. Said term may be extended for up to ten days and only once when the circumstances so justify it, and as long as a notification is provided to the data subject within the response term. When the exercise of ARCO rights is deemed to be correct, the responsible entity shall conduct within a term not exceeding fifteen days from the following day that the response has been notified to the data subject.

403. Article 55 establishes the criteria in twelve different sections when the exercise of ARCO rights shall not be possible.

404. Article 57 regulates data portability, and said article establishes that when personal data are processed electronically in a structured and commonly used format, the data subject will have the right to obtain from responsible entities a copy of the data that are being subject to processing in a structured and commonly used electronic format that allow data subjects to continue using it.

405. Title four consisting of Articles 58–64 is about the relation between responsible entities and parties under a specific legal mandate. Such title enlists the obligations regarding data processing of parties under a mandate and the conditions that the contract between the responsible entity and the parties under a specific mandate shall contain. Article 59 enlist the criteria for the clauses that said contract or legal instrument shall contain. Article 61 allows the mandated party to sublease services dealing with the processing of personal data as long as there is express authorization of the responsible entity under this law and other applicable regulations.

406. Article 63 allows responsible entities to enter into contracts or adhere to services, applications and infrastructure of cloud computing, and other matters that involve the processing of personal data, as long as the external cloud provider guarantees personal data protection policies equivalent to the established principles and duties contained in the GLPPDPGPSI and other provisions that are applicable to the subject matter.

407. Title Five of the GLPPDPGPSI consisting of Articles 65–71 establishes the rules for national and international transfers of personal data which are mainly conditioned to the consent of the data subject. All transfers of personal shall be materialized through the use of contractual standard clauses, collaboration agreements or any other legal instrument that allows the scope of processing of personal data, as well as obligations and responsibilities undertaken by both parties. Article 69 establishes the obligation of responsible entities to communicate and disclose the privacy notice to data subjects. Article 70 establishes the criteria in nine sections when the responsible party may transfer personal data without consent of the data subject. Article 71 establishes that national and international data transfers between responsible entities and parties under a legal mandate shall neither require notification to data subjects nor their consent.

408. Title Sixth of the GLPPDPGPSI consisting of Articles 72–79 establishes preventive actions and best practices on data protection. Article 72 allows responsible parties to develop or adopt, individually or in agreement with other responsible entities, parties under a mandate or organizations, best-practice schemes that aim to: (i) raise the level of protection of personal data; (ii) harmonize the processing of personal data in a specific sector; (iii) facilitate the exercise of ARCO rights by data subjects; (iv) facilitate the transfer of personal data; (v) complement the provisions set forth in the applicable regulations regarding the protection of personal data; and (vi) demonstrate before INAI or regulatory agencies the compliance with the regulations applicable to the area of protection of personal data.

409. Chapter II of Title Sixth of the GLPPDPGPSI consisting of Articles 80–82 regulates the processing of personal data by agencies and entities in charge of security, procurement and administration of justice, national security, public safety, or for the prevention or prosecution of crimes. Article 81 establishes that the processing of personal data as well as the use of databases for storage of information by agencies and entities in charge of security, procurement and administration of justice shall comply with the principles established under Title Second of the GLPPDPGPSI.

410. As of September 2021, INAI has issued more than seventeen guidelines and recommendations on data protection for public sector entities. These guidelines help to provide further guidance and interpretation of the GLPPDPGPSI for both responsible parties and data subjects.[109]

---

109. *See:* INAI, 'Documents and Guides for the Public Sector', available at: https://home.inai.org.mx/?page_id=3420.

Chapter 7. Data Protection in the Field of AI

411. Mexico was one of the first countries in Latin America to announce a national AI strategy in 2018. The national AI strategy was commissioned by the United Kingdom's Embassy in Mexico and developed in collaboration with the former Office of the Mexican President under the administration of Peña Nieto where a number of private sector entities, academia and civil society participated in its drafting.[110]

412. The current administration under President López Obrador (2018–2024) has neither implemented the goals outlined in the 2018 AI strategy nor the OECD AI Principles,[111] even though the Mexican government fully endorsed said principles in 2019, and it is one of the founding members of the Global Partnership on AI.[112] Likewise, Mexico has a representation at UNESCO's World Commission on the Ethics of Scientific Knowledge and Technology, which is currently working on the development of a Recommendation on the Ethics of AI.[113]

413. In the field of human rights and AI, the Mexican government through INAI was among the national data protection agencies that sponsored the GPA's *Resolution on Accountability in the Development and Use of Artificial Intelligence* during the forty-second GPA meeting in October 2020.[114]

Further, INAI, through the RIPD, sponsored and adopted a document titled: 'Specific Guidelines for Complying with the Principles and Rights Governing Personal Data Protection in Artificial Intelligence Projects' during the XVII meeting of the RIPD on 21 June 2019.[115]

---

110. *See:* Oxford Insights, British Embassy Mexico City and C-Minds, *Towards an AI Strategy in Mexico: Harnessing the AI Revolution* (June 2018), available at: https://docs.wixstatic.com/ugd/7be025_e726c582191c49d2b8b6517a590151f6.pdf.
111. *See*: OECD, *Recommendation of the Council on Artificial Intelligence*. Adopted on 21 May 2019, available at: https://legalinstruments.oecd.org/en/instruments/OECD-LEGAL-0449.
112. The Global Partnership on Artificial Intelligence (GPAI) is the first international AI partnership, which gathers experts from industry, government, civil society and academia to conduct research and develop AI policies and foster international cooperation, available at: https://gpai.ai/. *See*: OECD, 'OECD to host Secretariat of new Global Partnership on Artificial Intelligence', 15 Jun. 2020, available at: https://www.oecd.org/going-digital/ai/oecd-to-host-secretariat-of-new-global-partnership-on-artificial-intelligence.htm; and Secretaria de Relaciones Exteriores (SRE), 'Declaración Conjunta de los miembros fundadores de la Alianza Global sobre la Inteligencia Artificial', 15 Jun. 2020, available at: https://www.gob.mx/sre/prensa/declaracion-conjunta-de-los-miembros-fundadores-de-la-alianza-global-sobre-la-inteligencia-artificial.
113. *See* UNESCO, 'Elaboration of a Recommendation on the ethics of artificial intelligence', available at: https://en.unesco.org/artificial-intelligence/ethics.
114. Global Privacy Assembly (GPA), '*Adopted Resolution on Accountability in the Development and Use of Artificial Intelligence*', October 2020, available at: https://globalprivacyassembly.org/wp-content/uploads/2020/11/GPA-Resolution-on-Accountability-in-the-Development-and-Use-of-AI-EN.pdf.
115. Red Iberoamericana de Protección de Datos (RIPD), 'Orientaciones Específicas para el Cumplimiento de los Principios y Derechos que Rigen la Protección de los Datos Personales en los Proyectos de Inteligencia Artificial', 21 Jun. 2019. This document contains guidelines and recommendations addressed to data controllers and data processors for the processing of personal data in

414. INAI hosted the forty-third meeting of the GPA which as a result of COVID-19 took place virtually from 18–21 October 2021.[116] During this meeting, there was a keynote on the scope and limits of AI and a panel devoted to analyse the status of Convention 108+ and the prospect of a CoE treaty on AI, the latter of which analysed the ongoing work of the Council of Europe's Ad-hoc Committee on Artificial Intelligence[117] where the government of Mexico has an observatory status. During the conclusion of the forty-third meeting of the GPA, the Data Protection Commissioners elected INAI to serve as the Chair for the period 2021–2023.[118]

---

the context of systems and applications based on AI, available at: http://inicio.inai.org.mx/nuevo/RIPD_orientaciones_especificas_de_proteccion_de_datos_en_ia.pdf.

116. The programme of the 43rd meeting of the GPA is available at: https://gpamexico2021.org/about-gpa-copy-2/.
117. The website of the Council of Europe's Ad-hoc Committee on Artificial Intelligence (CAHAI) is available at: https://www.coe.int/en/web/artificial-intelligence/cahai#{%2266693378%22:[],%2266693401%22:[2],%2266693418%22:[1]}.
118. El Universal. Opinión de Josefina Román Vergara. 'La Asamblea Global de Privacidad: conclusiones y desafíos', 25 Oct. 2021, available at: https://bit.ly/3k9H3uQ.

Part XI. General Conclusions and Reflections

415. In the last decade, the right to personal data protection has had a significant impulse in the Mexican legal system. It is recognized as an autonomous human right, whose purpose is to safeguard privacy and the right to informational self-determination. This recognition has allowed the issuance of the FLPPDPP and the GLPPDPGPSI. It should also be considered that these advancements allowed Mexico to join the Convention 108 in 2018.

416. In addition to the specific legislation on the protection of personal data, for both the public and private sectors, there are currently more than forty-four federal laws that provide legal regulation regarding the processing of personal data in different sectors, such as education, health, financial, among others.

417. Likewise, in the last five years, the SCJN and the Federal Courts have considerably increased their case law regarding the protection of personal data in order to interpret the content and the scope of this human right, as well as its relationship with the enjoyment of other fundamental rights, such as the right to access to public information, the right to private life and the right to self-reputation. In some cases, the Supreme Court has extended the right to personal data to corporate entities with respect to confidentiality of their address and communications, economic, commercial or identity reports.

418. Additionally, the constitutional reform of 2014 strengthened the autonomy of the federal and state data protection authorities by recognizing their independence of the three branches of government (Executive, Legislative and Judicial), and establishing a national system that allows their coordination and collaboration to promote, protect and guarantee the right to personal data protection. This autonomy was reinforced by the Supreme Court in its decision to declare inadmissible the challenge of the INAI's decisions before the FCAJ. Currently, INAI's decisions can only be appealed through judicial courts.

419. The institutional strength of INAI has also impacted on the growing number of investigations and verification procedures, as well as on the amount of fines imposed on data controllers for non-compliance with the LFPPDPP. The sectors that have been subject to these procedures and sanctions to a greater extent are the professional, scientific and technical services, the financial and insurance sector, information in the mass media, the retail trade sector, and the health and social assistance sector. This information can be very useful for INAI, in order to reinforce the capacities of the most affected sectors in a more targeted approach.

420. However, there are asymmetries between the legislation of the public sector and the private sector. The GLPPDPGPSI, issued in January 2017, incorporates higher protection standards than the LFPPDPP, issued in July 2010, as the former takes the GDPR of the European Union as a reference. Some examples of these asymmetries can be observed in the fact that the LFPPDPP does not have provisions on the obligation to carry out privacy impact assessments under any circumstances, nor does it consider the figure of the data protection officer. In addition, the LFPPDPP lacks provisions on security breach notifications. The latter is one of the principal aspects that requires the most attention when reforming the law in order to incorporate a mandatory security breach notification system.

421. The FLPPDPP and its Regulation have little more than a decade of being in force. We strongly believe this framework needs an urgent modernization in order to reflect and balance the policies and recommendations of international organizations like the OECD, APEC and the CoE, as well as to mirror ongoing developments of technological trends like AI and the Internet of Things, whose main services and applications rely on the collection and processing of massive amounts of data and personal information of individuals.

422. The pending reform of the FLPPDPP and its Regulation may be an opportunity to raise the standards of personal data protection in the digital environment. At least two aspects that we consider to be priorities should be taken into account: (1) the lack of regulation regarding cookies, and (2) the problems faced by personal data authorities to guarantee the continuity of the protection when the information is processed beyond national borders.

423. Currently, the INAI has issued some guidelines for the use of cookies. However, these rules are not binding. It would be desirable to incorporate them into data protection legislation in order to give legal certainty to both data controllers and data subjects.

424. Additionally, the jurisdiction of the INAI and the applicable law on data protection are subject to territorial ties or to the formalization of contractual relations. This is problematic in those cases in which personal data is collected by international companies that do not have a representation office in Mexico. Furthermore, the international transfers regime is insufficient to solve this situation.

425. Technological advancements make it imperative to carry out a constant review of the regulations regarding personal data protection. In this context, we consider that it is necessary to incorporate into legislation and regulation the principles and rights contained in major international instruments on AI, including the OECD principles on AI addressed in the *OECD Recommendation of the OECD Council on Artificial Intelligence of 2019*, among other relevant international instruments.

426. The ongoing legal and policy development in the field of AI, like the recent Regulation proposal on AI of the European Union and the policies and recommendations in this area emerging from international organization like the OECD, the G7, UNESCO and the CoE, will have a significant impact in the regulation of privacy and data protection in many countries in the short term. Mexico should consider amending the legal frameworks on data protection for the private and public sector taking into account said legal and public policy developments and recommendation of the international organizations.

427. The provisions concerning the collection and processing of personal data by police, law enforcement authorities and intelligence entities contained in the national legislation should be revisited in order to strengthen and safeguard the protection of fundamental human rights of victims of crimes, including serious crimes like terrorism, sexual exploitation of children, organized crime and cybercrime.

428. It should be noted that legislative and regulatory progress is necessary but not sufficient conditions to safeguard the right to personal data protection. Further efforts are needed to reach adequate implementation and enforcement of the law. Recent cases, such as the use of the software PEGASUS by former PGR officials against journalists, activists and academics on behalf of national security, highlight the need to go beyond the mere formal recognition of the principles and rights of personal data subjects, obligations and procedures regarding personal data protection.

Selected Bibliography

Articles from Legal Journals, Magazines, News and Websites

Artículo 19, R3D and SOCIAL TIC, 'Gobierno Espía. Vigilancia Sistemática a periodistas y defensores de derechos humanos en México', June 2017.

Blanca Lilia Ibarra Cadena, 'México No Necesita un Gobierno Espía', La Silla Rota, 25 February 2019.

Council of Europe, 'Data Protection Day 2021 in Latin America. 40th Anniversary of data protection Convention 108'.

El Financiero, 'Telefónica México obtiene certificado en materia de protección de datos', 13 August, 2015.

El País, 'El Gobierno mexicano declaro secretos los contratos sobre el "software" del espionaje a periodistas', 21 June 2017.

El País, 'La Fiscalía de México ha contratado en los dos últimos años programas para el espionaje masivo de teléfonos móviles', 14 April 2021.

El Universal. Opinión de Josefina Román Vergara. 'La Asamblea Global de Privacidad: conclusiones y desafíos', 25 October 2021.

Gribakov, Andrei, 'Cross-Border Privacy Rules in Asia: An Overview'. Lawfare blog, 3 January 2019.

Global Privacy Assembly (GPA), '*Adopted Resolution on Accountability in the Development and Use of Artificial Intelligence*', October 2020.

Global Tax News, 'Mexico Participates in APEC Cross-Border Privacy System', 17 January 2013.

New York Times in Spanish, 'Somos los nuevos enemigos del Estado: el espionaje a activistas y periodistas en Mexico', 19 June 2017.

OECD, 'OECD to Host Secretariat of New Global Partnership on Artificial Intelligence', 15 June 2020.

Oxford Insights, British Embassy Mexico City and C-Minds, *Towards an AI Strategy in Mexico: Harnessing the AI Revolution,* June 2018.

Red en Defensa de los Derechos Digitales (R3D), '!Ganamos! Tribunal anula resolución del INAI sobre el falso derecho al olvido', 24 August 2016.

Red en Defensa de los Derechos Digitales (R3D), 'El Estado de la Vigilancia. Fuera de Control', November 2016.

Red Iberoamericana de Protección de Datos (RIPD), 'Orientaciones Específicas para el Cumplimiento de los Principios y Derechos que Rigen la Protección de los Datos Personales en los Proyectos de Inteligencia Artificial', 21 June 2019.

Selected Bibliography

Documents and Reports from Government, Industry and Academia

Government

Senado de la República. Coordinación de Comunicación Social, 'La Constitución Política de México es una de las mas reformadas en el mundo, señala el IBD', 27 October 2018.
Secretaría de Relaciones Exteriores (SRE), 'Declaración Conjunta de los miembros fundadores de la Alianza Global sobre la Inteligencia Artificial', 15 June 2020.

International Treaties and Agreements

American Declaration of Rights and Duties of Mankind (1948).
Charter of Fundamental Rights of the European Union.
General Agreement on Trade in Services (GATS).
The American Convention on Human Rights adopted on 22 November 1969.
The Convention on the Rights of the Children (1989).
The Comprehensive and Progressive Agreement for Trans-Pacific Partnership signed on 8 March 2018.
The Council of Europe Convention for the Protection of Individuals with regards to the Automatic Processing of Personal Data (Convention 108).
The Council of Europe Modernized Convention for the Protection of Individuals with regards to the Automatic Processing of Personal Data and Explanatory Report (Convention 108+).
The Economic Partnership, Political Coordination and Cooperation Agreement between the European Community and its Member States, of the one part, and the United Mexican States, of the other part adopted by the EU Council on 28 September 2000.
The International Pact of Civil and Political Rights (1966).
The International Convention on the Protection of the Rights of All Migrant Workers and Members of Their Families (1990).
US-Mexico-Canada Trade Agreement (USMCA).
Universal Declaration of Human Rights (1948).

Foreign Laws and Regulations

Directive 95/46/EC of the European Parliament and of the Council of 24 October 1995 on the protection of individuals with regard to the processing of personal data and on the free movement of such data.
Directive (EU) 2016/680 of the European Parliament and of the Council of 27 April 2016 on the protection of natural persons with regard to the processing of personal data by competent authorities for the purposes of the prevention, investigation, detection or prosecution of criminal offences or the execution of criminal penalties, and on the free movement of such data, and repealing Council Framework Decision 2008/977/JHA.
Ley Orgánica 7/2021, de 26 de mayo, de protección de datos personales tratados para fines de prevención, detección, investigación y enjuiciamiento de infracciones penales y de ejecución de sanciones penales published in BOE number 126 of 27 May 2021.
Proposal of the EC Regulation on Privacy and Electronic Communications.

Regulation (EU) 2016/679 of the European Parliament and of the Council of 27 April 2016 on the protection of natural persons with regard to the processing of personal data and on the free movement of such data, and repealing Directive 95/46/EC (General Data Protection Regulation).

Guidelines, Recommendations and Documents of International Organizations

APEC Privacy Framework (2015).
APEC Cross-Border Privacy Rules System.
International Standards on the Protection of Personal Data Protection and Privacy (The Madrid Resolution of November 2009).
CJI, *Updated Principles on Privacy and the Personal Data Protection, with Annotations*. Approved on April 2021.
OECD, *Recommendation of the Council on Artificial Intelligence*. Adopted on 21 May 2019.
The OECD Revised Guidelines on the Protection of Privacy and Transborder Flows of Personal Data (2013).
UNESCO, 'Elaboration of a Recommendation on the ethics of artificial intelligence'.
United Nations Guidelines for the Regulation of Computerized Personal Data Files of 21 July 1988.

Judgments and Opinions of Foreign Courts

Court of Justice of the European Union (CJEU), *Google Spain v. AEPD, Mario Costeja Gonzalez* of 13 May 2014.
Inter-American Court of Human Rights. Advisory Opinion OC-24/17 of 24 November 20117, Series A No. 24.
Inter-American Court of Human Rights. Case of *Cesti-Hurtado v. Peru*, Judgment of 29 September 1999, paragraph 177.
Inter-American Court of Human Rights. Case of the *Gómez Paquiyauri Brothers v. Peru*, Judgment of 8 July 2004, p. 182.
Inter-American Court of Human Rights. Case of *Cesti-Hurtado v. Peru*, Judgment of 29 September 1999 (Merits), paragraph 177.
Inter-American Court of Human Rights. Case *Bueno Alves v. Argentina*, Judgment of 11 May 2007, paragraph 122.
Inter-American Court of Human Rights Case *Valle Jaramillo et al. v. Colombia*, Judgment of 27 November 2008, paragraph 176.
Inter-American Court of Human Rights. Case of *Escué-Zapata v. Colombia*, Judgment of 4 July 2007 (Merits, Reparations and Costs), paragraph 91
Inter-American Court of Human Rights. Case *Fernández Ortega et al. v. Mexico*, Judgment of 30 August 2010, paragraph 129.
Inter-American Court of Human Rights. Case *Fernández Prieto and Tumbeiro v. Argentina*, Judgment of 1 September 2020, paragraph 102.
Inter-American Court of Human Rights. Case of the *Ituango Massacres v. Colombia*, Judgment of 1 July 2006 (Preliminary Objections, Merits, Reparations and Costs), paragraph 193.
Inter-American Court of Human Rights. Case of *Tristán Donoso v. Panama*, Judgment of 27 January 2009, paragraph 55.

Selected Bibliography

Inter-American Court of Human Rights. *Escher et al. v. Brazil*, Judgment of 6 July 2009, paragraph 113.
Inter-American Court of Human Rights. Case *Fernández Prieto and Tumbeiro v. Argentina*, Judgment of 1 September 2020, paragraph 102.
Inter-American Court of Human Rights. Case of *Escher et al. v. Brazil*, Judgment of 6 July 2009, paragraph 114.
Inter-American Court of Human Rights. Case of *Rosendo Cantú v. Mexico*, Judgment of 31 August 2010, paragraph 119.
Inter-American Court of Human Rights. Case of the *Ituango Massacres v. Colombia*, Judgment of 1 July 2006 (Preliminary Objections, Merits, Reparations and Costs), paragraph 195.
Inter-American Court of Human Rights. Case of *Guachalá Chimbo et al. v. Ecuador*, Judgment of 26 March 2021, paragraph 110.
Inter-American Court of Human Rights. Case of *López et al. v. Argentina*, Judgment of 25 November 2019, paragraph 97.
Inter-American Court of Human Rights. Case of *I.V. v. Bolivia*, Judgment of 30 November 2016, paragraph 122.
Inter-American Court of Human Rights. Case of *Artavia Murillo et al. v. Costa Rica*, Judgment of 28 November 2012, paragraph 143.

Federal Laws, Codes and Regulations

Political Constitution of the Mexican United States.
Advanced Electronic Signature Law.
Code of Commerce.
Federal Civil Code.
Federal Code of Civil Procedure.
Federal Code of Institutions and Electoral Proceedings.
Federal Consumer Protection Law.
Federal Criminal Code.
Federal Electricity Commission Law.
Federal Labour Law.
Federal Law of Administrative Procedure.
Federal Law of Public Commission.
Federal Law Against Organized Crime.
Federal Law for the Protection of Industrial Property
Federal Law of Authors Right.
Federal Law of Economic Competition.
Federal Law of Telecommunications and Broadcasting.
Federal Law of Transparency and Access to Public Information.
Federal Law of the Rights of Contributor.
Federal Law on Protection of Personal Data Held by Private Parties.
Fiscal Code of the Federation.
Foreign Investment Law.
General Archives Law.
General Health Law.
General Law of Administrative Responsibilities.
General Law of Education.

General Law of Electoral Institutions and Procedures.
General Law of Population.
General Law of the National Public Security System.
General Law of Transparency and Access to Public Government Information.
General Law on Forced Disappearance of Persons, Disappearance Committed by Individuals and the National Missing Persons Search System.
General Law on Protection of Personal Data in Possession of Government and Public Sector Institutions.
Geographic and Statistics Information Law.
Industrial Property Law.
Investment Funds Law.
Investment Partnerships Law.
Law of Administrative Liability of Public Servants.
Law of Audit and Accountability of the Federation.
Law of Credit Institutions.
Law of Public Commission.
Law of the Bank of Mexico.
Law of the National System of Statistical and Geographic Information.
Law of the Institute for Security and Social Services for State Workers.
Law of the Professional Carrier Service in the Federal Public Administration.
Law on Crimes of the Press.
Law on Migration.
Law on Refugees, Complementary Protection and Political Asylum.
Law on Savings and Popular Credit.
Law for the Promotion of Citizen Confidence.
Law for the Protection and Defense of the User of Financial Services.
Law for the Regulation of Article 5 of the Federal Constitution Pertaining to the Practice of Professions in the Federal District.
Law to Regulate Credit Information Partnerships.
National Code of Criminal Procedure.
National Security Law.
Saving and Popular Credit Law.
Securities Market Law.
Social Security Law.

Regulations

Regulation of the Federal Law of Transparency and Access to Public Government Information.
Regulation of the Federal Law on Protection of Personal Data Held by Private Parties.
Regulation of the National Electoral Institute on Protection of Personal Data.
Regulatory Law of Article 5 of the Constitution.

Selected Bibliography

Decrees, Guidelines and Official Standards

Decreto Promulgatorio de la Presidencia de la República published in DOF on 28 September 2018.

General Guidelines for Access, Rectification, Cancellation and Opposition to Personal Data which are part of INE's Electoral List.

General Guidelines for Document and Information Requests made under Article 126 section 3 of the General Law of Institutions and Electoral Proceedings;

General Guidelines for the access, verification and disclosure of personal data in possession of the Executive Direction of the Federal Electoral Registry by the members of the General, Local and District Councils, the Oversight Commissions of the Federal Register of Voters and the Local Public Bodies.

Agreement of the General Council of the National Electoral Institute, by which the implementation of the verification service of the data of the Voting Card is approved, which will serve to safeguard the right to data protection of citizens contained in the Electoral Register.

National Official Norm on Medical Records (NOM-004-SSA3-2012) published in DOF on 15 October 2012.

Judgments and Resolutions of the SCJN and Federal Courts in Mexico

Seventh Collegiate Court on Administrative Matters of the First Circuit, Ninth Epoch, Register 180940, Thesis I.7o.A.312 A, Federal Weekly Judiciary Gazette, Volume XX, August 2004, p. 1565.

Fourth Collegiate Court on Administrative Matters of the First Circuit, Ninth Epoch, Register 160980, Thesis I.4o.A.790 A, Federal Weekly Judiciary Gazette, Volume XXXIV, September 2011, p. 2244.

Plenary of Circuits on Administrative Matters of the First Circuit, Tenth Epoch, Register 2006753, Jurisprudence PC.I.A. J/12 K (10a.), Federal Weekly Judiciary Gazette, Book 7, Volume II, June 2014, p. 1127.

Third Collegiate Court on Civil and Work Matters of the Fifth Circuit, Tenth Epoch, Register 2021523, Thesis V.3o.C.T.10 K (10a.), Federal Weekly Judiciary Gazette, Book 74, Volume III, January 2020, p. 2445.

National Supreme Court of Justice, Tenth Epoch, Register 2022917, Jurisprudence 2a./J. 10/2021 (10a.), Federal Weekly Judiciary Gazette, Book 84, Volume II, March 2021, p. 1651.

Tenth Collegiate Court on Administrative Matters of the First Circuit, Tenth Epoch, Register 2020563, Thesis I.10o.A.5.CS (10a.), Federal Weekly Judiciary Gazette, Book 70, Volume III, September 2019, p. 2199.

Third Collegiate Court of the Thirteenth Circuit, Ninth Epoch, Register 176077, Thesis XIII.3o.12 A, Federal Weekly Judiciary Gazette, Volume XXIII, January 2006, p. 2518.

National Supreme Court of Justice, Ninth Epoch, Register 169167, Thesis 2a. XCIX/2008, Federal Weekly Judiciary Gazette, Volume XXVIII, July 2008, p. 549.

National Supreme Court of Justice, Tenth Epoch, Register 2005521, Thesis P. I/2014, Federal Weekly Judiciary Gazette, Book 3, Volume I, February 2014, p. 273.

National Supreme Court of Justice, Tenth Epoch, Register 2005522, Thesis P. II/2014 (10a.), Federal Weekly Judiciary Gazette, Book 3, Volume I, February 2014, p. 274.

First Collegiate Court on Administrative Matters of the First Circuit, Specialized in Economic Competition, Broadcasting and Telecommunications, Tenth Epoch, Register 2011916, Thesis I.1o.A.E.159 A, Federal Weekly Judiciary Gazette, Book 31, Volume IV, June 2016, p. 2872.

National Supreme Court of Justice, Tenth Epoch, Register 2000233 Thesis 1a. VII/2012 (10a.), Federal Weekly Judiciary Gazette, Book V, Volume I, February 2012, p. 655.

Plenary of Circuits on Administrative Matters of the First Circuit, Tenth Epoch, Register 2020687, Jurisprudence PC.I.A. J/153 A (10a.), Federal Weekly Judiciary Gazette, Book 70, Volume II, September 2019, p. 1340.

Tenth Collegiate Court on Administrative Matters of the First Circuit, Tenth Epoch, Register 2020549, Thesis I.10o.A.120. A (10a.), Federal Weekly Judiciary Gazette, Book 70, Volume III, September 2019, p. 1853.

National Supreme Court of Justice, Ninth Epoch, Register 192867, Thesis P. LXXXVII/99, Federal Weekly Judiciary Gazette Volume X, November 1999.

SCJN, Contradicción de Tesis 293/2011, Pleno, Min. Arturo Zaldívar, resolución del 3 de septiembre de 2013.

SCJN, Tesis 1ª./J. 29/2015 (10ª.), *Gaceta del Semanario Judicial de la Federación*, Libro 17, Abril de 2015, Tomo I, p. 240.

National Supreme Court of Justice, Tenth Epoch, Register 2022203, Jurisprudence 2a./J. 31/2020 (10a.), Federal Weekly Judiciary Gazette, Book I, Volume II, October 2020, p. 668.

Guidelines and Documents of INAI

INAI Finding File Number PPD.0094/14 Google México S. de R.L. de C.V.

INAI, 'Guía para Titulares de Datos Personales. Volumen 3. Los Derechos Arcos'.

INAI, 'Guía para Titulares de los Datos Personales Volumen 4. Procedimientos de Datos Personales ante el INAI'.

INAI, 'Recommendations for the Management of Security Breaches of Personal Data', June 2018.

INAI, 'Recommendations for the Appointment of the Person or Department responsible for Data Protection', August 2016.

Privacy Notice Guidelines (Lineamientos del Aviso de Privacidad) published in DOF on 17 January 2013.

Ministry of Economy, 'Self-Regulation Standards on Protection of Personal Data' published in DOF of 29 May 2014.

General Guidelines for the implementation of Compensatory Measures without express authorization published in DOF on 18 April 2012.

INAI Prepared Activity Reports of 2019 and 2020 submitted to the Senate of the Mexican Union Congress.

INAI, 'Multas impuestas en 2020 por Infracciones a la Ley Federal de Protección de Datos Personales suman más de 39 MDP: INAI. Comunicado INAI/011/21', Ciudad de México, 10 January 2021.

Selected Bibliography

INAI. ‘Determina INAI que FGR incumplió la Ley General de Protección de Datos Personales en Posesión de Sujetos Obligados’. Comunicado del INAI/054/19 of 20 February 2019.

INAI, ‘Documents and Guides for the Public Sector’.

Websites

APEC Cross-Border Privacy Rule System, http://cbprs.org/.

Artículo 19.Org, https://articulo19.org/.

Asia-Pacific Economic Cooperation (APEC), https://www.apec.org/.

Boletín Oficial del Estado del Gobierno de España, https://www.boe.es/.

Cámara de Diputados LXV Legislatura del H. Congreso de la Unión, http://www.diputados.gob.mx/.

Corte Interamericana de Derechos Humanos, https://www.corteidh.or.cr/.

Council of Europe, https://www.coe.int/.

Council of Europe’s Ad-hoc Committee on Artificial Intelligence (CAHAI),https://www.coe.int/en/web/artificial-intelligence/cahai#{%2266693378%22:[],%2266693401%22:[2],%2266693418%22:[1]}.

Diario Oficial de la Federación (DOF), https://www.dof.gob.mx/.

El País, https://elpais.com/.

El Universal, https://www.eluniversal.com.mx.

Foreign Trade Information System of the Organization of American States (SICE), http://www.sice.oas.org/.

Global Partnership on Artificial Intelligence (GPAI), https://gpai.ai/.

Global Privacy Assembly (GPA), https://globalprivacyassembly.org/.

Ibero-American Data Protection Network (RIPD), https://www.redipd.org/es.

Instituto Belisario Domínguez del Senado de la República, http://ibd.senado.gob.mx/.

Instituto Nacional Electoral (INE), https://www.ine.mx/.

Inter-American Court of Human Rights, https://www.corteidh.or.cr f.

La Silla Rota, https://lasillarota.com.

Mexico’s National System of Transparency, Access to Public Information and Protection of Personal Data, http://www.snt.org.mx/.

New York Times in Spanish, https://www.nytimes.com/spotlight/read-the-times-in-spanish.

Suprema Corte de Justicia de la Nación de México, https://www.scjn.gob.mx/.

Organization for Economic Cooperation and Development (OECD), https://www.oecd.org/.

OECD Legal Instruments, https://legalinstruments.oecd.org/en/.

Red en Defensa de los Derechos Digitales (R3D), https://r3d.mx/.

Sello de Confianza de la Asociación de Internet.mx, https://sellosdeconfianza.org.mx/index.php.

World Trade Organization, https://www.wto.org/.

Index

The numbers here refer to paragraph numbers.

Index

www.ingramcontent.com/pod-product-compliance
Ingram Content Group UK Ltd.
Pitfield, Milton Keynes, MK11 3LW, UK
UKHW020143290926
15471UKWH00004B/675

9 789403 507163